ROYAL BLOOMS

This edition published in 2025 by Welbeck
An Imprint of HEADLINE PUBLISHING GROUP LIMITED

1

Cataloguing in Publication Data is available from the British Library

ISBN 978-1-03542-342-2

Printed in China by C & C Offset Printing Co., Ltd.

FSC www.fsc.org MIX Paper | Supporting responsible forestry FSC® C104740

Headline's policy is to use papers that are natural, renewable and recyclable products and made from wood grown in well-managed forests and other controlled sources. The logging and manufacturing processes are expected to conform to the environmental regulations of the country of origin.

HEADLINE PUBLISHING GROUP LIMITED
An Hachette UK Company
Carmelite House
50 Victoria Embankment
London EC4Y 0DZ

The authorised representative in the EEA is Hachette Ireland,
8 Castlecourt Centre, Dublin 15, D15 XTP3,
Ireland (email: info@hbgi.ie)

www.headline.co.uk
www.hachette.co.uk

HISTORIC ROYAL PALACES

ROYAL BLOOMS

THE CROWN AND PLANTS: A VERY NOBLE HISTORY

FELICITY DAY

Contents

Foreword

In March 1554, the future Queen Elizabeth I was arrested on suspicion of conspiring against her half-sister 'Bloody' Mary Tudor. She was imprisoned in the Tower, in the very same apartments where her mother Anne Boleyn had been lodged prior to her execution eighteen years earlier. Terrified that she would meet the same fate, Elizabeth was said to have begged her sister to order a sword for her beheading – a privilege that Henry VIII had afforded Anne. But although public sympathy was firmly with the captive princess, the Tower Constable was dismissed from his post because he was considered too lenient towards her.

One day, when Elizabeth was taking her daily exercise along the Tower walkway, a young boy, overcome with curiosity, struck up a conversation with her. It was the beginning of an unlikely friendship and they met several more times as the princess's imprisonment dragged on. Charmed by his royal friend, the boy started bringing her flowers. When Mary's privy council heard of this, they ordered that the boy be kept away from their royal captive.

But those simple blooms had already worked their magic. To Elizabeth, they were a glimmer of hope during one of the bleakest periods of her life: a testament to the love that she inspired among her sister's ordinary subjects. She was eventually released on 19 May 1554, the anniversary of her mother's execution, and crowned Queen of England four and a half years later. Now, the love that those flowers had represented found full expression. The citizens of London cheered the new queen as she returned to the Tower in triumph to await her coronation. As she processed through the streets thronged with well-wishers, thousands of flowers were thrown into her path.

As this wonderful book reveals, throughout history, monarchs have had a special connection with plants. From the *planta genista* (sprig of bloom) that inspired the name of a medieval royal dynasty to the honeysuckle that proudly (but falsely) proclaimed the constancy of Henry VIII's love for Anne Boleyn, and from the fragrant orange trees that Mary II filled Hampton Court with in the late 17th century to the gentian and other medicinal plants used to treat the so-called 'madness' of King George III, the British monarchy has proved surprisingly green-fingered.

The story of the monarchy has been told and retold many times, but reading this book gave me a perspective as fresh as the beautifully decorated firs which were first brought into the palaces by George III's consort Charlotte every Christmas, thus beginning a tradition that is still going strong today.

It is a centuries-old story but one that continues to evolve. In May 2023, Westminster Abbey was filled with trees, flowers and foliage for the coronation of King Charles III. And each year, tens of thousands of visitors flock to palaces such as Hampton Court, Kensington and Hillsborough Castle to enjoy the gardens, just as much as the majestic buildings.

From showy delphiniums to the humble cowslip and everything in between, *Royal Blooms* is bursting with colour – and history. The monarchy might be known for its material splendour, but as the 17th-century philosopher and abolitionist Ralph Waldo Emerson observed: 'Flowers are a proud assertion that a ray of beauty outvalues all the utilities in the world.' I'm sure even Henry VIII would agree.

Tracy Borman
Chief Historian, Historic Royal Palaces

Introduction

The coronation of King Charles III in May 2023 had all the pomp and pageantry you could ask for: a gold coach, velvet robes and jewel-encrusted crowns, ceremonial trumpeters and the country's most historic chair. But among it all was also a proliferation of plants. Trees guarded the entrance to Westminster Abbey, and from the high altar to the grave of the unknown warrior, the Abbey itself was bursting with home-grown flowers and foliage; plants formed the coronation emblem, adorned the invitations and embellished the Queen's Robe of Estate, their presence everywhere proclaiming the new sovereign's passion for Britain's natural treasures. If Charles I was 'the martyr king' and Charles II 'the merry monarch', then Charles III was very clearly going to be our 'green king'. More than one writer dubbed him 'Hortulanus Rex', and many declared him the most green-fingered monarch in our history.

Yet the truth is, plants have been special to many more sovereigns than Charles in the centuries past, and, in fact, have been closely entwined with the Crown for almost as long as our monarchy has existed – from great, tall oaks to tiny forget-me-nots, and from gnarled, old yews to fragrant herbs, Britain's flora has always been a part of the royal story.

Plants have been silent witnesses to moments that have changed the course of history. They have helped royals to keep hold of the crown, saved them from harm and provided solace in times of crisis. As emblems and envoys, they have carried unspoken messages. They have been used for political ends, to celebrate and commemorate, and simply to show off. Plants that, to us, are purely decorative have been deployed (with varying success) to treat ailing monarchs, and have featured in the lavish dishes laid out on their groaning royal dinner tables.

ABOVE
Flowers like violets have been royal emblems and envoys, used by Kings and Queens to celebrate, commemorate and show-off. 'Viola odorata' by Maggie Hatherley-Champ, 2013.

This book, illustrated with botanical drawings, portraits and photographs, many of which are from the archives of Historic Royal Palaces, sets out to tell some of those stories; to bring the part played in royal history by various plants and flowers from the shade of the garden into the splendour of the palace, and into the lives of the royals who inhabited those palaces.

It does not attempt to cover species or cultivation, for many words have been written on those subjects by many more knowledgeable minds. And it cannot claim to be anywhere near exhaustive, not least because plants are so often in the background, part of the everyday existence at court that those in centuries past never thought to record on paper. Portraits and possessions, letters, recipes and the like sometimes give us clues, but frustratingly little in the way of detail.

What this volume can do, by rolling back through the reigns and following Charles' many predecessors up the garden path, is remind us that the royal passion for plants did not begin with our green king and undoubtedly will continue for many generations to come.

OPPOSITE
King Charles and Queen Camilla return from Westminster Abbey in the Gold State Coach on the day of their coronation.

ABIES

FIR

-

Every year, millions of Britons bring a real fir tree into their homes at Christmas time, and for that we have the royals to thank.

THE TRADITION OF DECORATING FIRS AND OTHER EVERGREENS to mark the festive season is an old German one, dating back to at least the early 1600s. Contrary to popular opinion, it was not Prince Albert who first introduced his British relations to the custom, but his wife's grandmother, Queen Charlotte – though that was a yew tree rather than a fir. The consort of King George III was born and raised in the small German duchy of Mecklenburg-Strelitz, and as a child had always decorated a single yew branch at Christmas, which her family gathered around to exchange gifts. She brought her family tradition with her to England on her marriage to George in 1761, and by 1800 was decorating entire trees at court, usually as the centrepiece for Christmas parties for children. One, a fir 'about as high again as any of us, lighted all over' and bedecked with 'strings of almonds and raisins' was, reported courtier Georgina Townshend, 'heartily' enjoyed by her young guests.

Though this tradition remained unfamiliar to the greater part of the British population, the wider Royal Family came to cherish trees as part of their yuletide festivities from then on. In the 1830s, Charlotte's daughter-in-law Queen Adelaide set up enormous trees, groaning with gilded fruits and nuts, in the banqueting room at the Royal Pavilion in Brighton, where she and her husband King William IV often spent the festive season. And at her home in Kensington Palace, a young Princess Victoria had Christmas trees 'hung with lights

OPPOSITE
Victoria, Albert and their family gather around a twinkling Christmas tree at Windsor Castle by J.L. Williams, 1848.

and sugar ornaments' and placed on a round table, with her presents laid out invitingly underneath. She was only permitted to see them when her Mama rang a bell late in the afternoon on Christmas Eve, when, in line with German custom, the family exchanged their gifts (as the royals still do today).

With Albert, Victoria kept up the tradition at Windsor Castle, where they spent all twenty-one of their Christmases together. Amid its gilded splendour, they set up copious trees: one each, one for the children, one for the courtiers, and one for the servants, most on tables like Victoria's early ones, though they were known to create a spectacle by replacing some of the castle's chandeliers with trees hung from the ceiling too.

Specially imported from the Prince's native Coburg, their fir trees – some 'of immense size' – were decorated with frosting to imitate fallen snow, as well as an abundance of candles, which were lit only on Christmas Eve. The royal children could be sent into 'ecstasies' at the very sight of them. For the Queen, their smell was the scent of 'pleasant memories'.

Illustrations of the couple's twinkling trees began to appear in the press from the 1840s onwards, and it was then that the Christmas tree really caught the imagination of the nation at large. Victoria and Albert helped the custom to take root by gifting trees from their estates to schools, hospitals and army barracks, a practice which continues in a similar form today. The King presents fir trees to churches including Westminster Abbey, St Paul's Cathedral and Edinburgh's Canongate Kirk, and also to schools in the Sandringham area, just as his mother always did.

Privately, however, the modern royals do Christmas rather less lavishly than Queen Victoria, who even as an ageing widow liked richly trimmed trees by the dozen dotted around Osborne House on the Isle of Wight. Trees remain an indispensable part of their festivities, of course, but at Sandringham there have usually been just two. One for the household and another for the family, the latter reportedly a magnificent 20-ft specimen, grown on the estate and placed in the White Drawing Room. The late Queen liked her youngest relatives to help finish decorating it.

In 2023, the King delivered his second Christmas Broadcast alongside a living tree, which was briefly uprooted and destined to be replanted in the New Year – his new and characteristically sustainable spin on this old and treasured royal tradition.

OPPOSITE
A Christmas tree at St Paul's Cathedral, London, 1953.

ABOVE
King Charles delivered his Christmas message in front of a living tree in 2023.

OPPOSITE
Each year, Christmas trees grown on the royal estates are presented to a number of churches around Britain.

15

Althaea rosea Cav.

Alcea

Hollyhock

Legend has it that this cottage garden favourite, the tall and jolly hollyhock, was introduced to England by an intrepid English Queen, Eleanor of Castile, on her return from a crusade in the Holy Land.

The truth of the tale is hard to verify. Spanish Princess Eleanor and the future King Edward I were wed as teenagers in 1254, a marriage of diplomatic convenience that, in their case, turned into a love match. When Edward departed on crusade sixteen years later, Eleanor certainly accompanied him to Palestine, where she gave birth for perhaps the eighth time. And hollyhocks, native to China but growing in the Middle East by then, are certainly believed to have arrived in England around the late 13th century – at the very least, long before their first mention in writing here in around 1440. The flower's common name – a combination of the religious 'holy' with '*hoc*', the Anglo-Saxon word for mallow, to which family it belongs – adds some credence to the theory that it arrived with returning crusaders, if not with Eleanor.

There's no doubt, too, that the strong-willed and intelligent Queen was an interested and informed gardener, intent on creating oases of green wherever she was to reside. Gardens were conjured from scratch in anticipation of stays at Caernarfon and Rhuddlan castles in Wales. She supervised the replanting of the royal garden at Westminster with vines, roses and a herbarium, and lavished attention – and no doubt expense – on the garden of the manor she owned at Langley in Hertfordshire, where the gardeners she employed were brought over from her native Spain.

OPPOSITE
A 19th-century illustration of the hollyhock flower by Walther Muller, 1887.

BELOW
Legend says that Eleanor saved Edward's life on crusade by sucking the poison from a wound inflicted by an assassin. 'Eleanor Sucking the Venom out of the Wound of her Husband King Edward I' by Angelica Kauffman, c. 1780.

OPPOSITE
Stone statues of Edward I and his Queen, Eleanor of Castile, on the exterior of Lincoln Cathedral. The first recorded mention of these statues is 1280.

Whether Eleanor's gardens had stately hollyhocks or not we can't say for sure. If they were there, they probably belonged in her herb garden, because of their purported healing qualities; hollyhocks have long been considered anti-inflammatory.

What the Queen's gardens definitely did have was quince trees. Pining for a taste of her Spanish home, she is said to have had them brought over to England specially to make *mermelada*, or quince jam. Records show four saplings being planted at the Tower of London in 1275, not long after her return from the crusade. They cost more than the one hundred cherry trees purchased at the same time, proving quinces – which are a bit like pears, only harder and far more bitter – to be a luxury that few but a medieval Queen could afford.

ABOVE
Illustration of a medieval garden: 'The Prisoners Listening to Emily Singing in the Garden' by Giovanni Boccaccio, 1340–41.

OPPOSITE
A 19th-century illustration of a quince tree and fruit by Augusta Withers, 1857.

Pl. VII.
Dec. VIII.
Pyrus Cydonia. Linn.
Coignassier
Mille 2.
Cent 2.
Dupin fil.

Ananas. Tourn. 653. An Ananas sylvestris, minor? seu Ananas altera, minor.

Ananas comosus

Pineapple

In the 17th and 18th centuries, a pineapple, being notoriously costly and very tricky to cultivate, was the ultimate status symbol, so naturally the so-called 'king of fruits' found a place on the royal table.

EUROPE'S VERY FIRST PINEAPPLE PLANT came back from the Americas with Christopher Columbus in 1496, but the first British monarch to sample the sweet and spiky fruit was Charles II, who enjoyed a prized specimen that was brought to his table from Barbados in the summer of 1661.

It was not the first pineapple ever seen in England, however, for that had reportedly been presented to Charles' nemesis, Oliver Cromwell, four years earlier. But pineapple was still an incredibly rare and exotic foodstuff, and whenever the opportunity subsequently arose to show off his access to it, the fashion-forward King did not fail to take it. In 1668, a pineapple made a very public appearance on his table at a dinner given for the French ambassador in the Palace of Whitehall's Banqueting Hall, when the ceremonial carving and tasting of it served not just as a talking point, but as a reminder of England's growing power in the West Indies. Then, in the 1670s, the 'Merry Monarch' agreed to be painted with a pineapple, which, thanks to the 'crown' of leaves upon its head, had become irrevocably associated with royalty, so becoming the 'king' of all fruits.

The painting, in which Charles is reverently presented with a somewhat lacklustre specimen by the royal gardener John Rose, was for a long time said to have been a celebration

OPPOSITE
Illustration of a growing pineapple by Giovanni Battista Morandi from *Hortulus botanicus pictus sive collectio plantarum*, 1748.

of the first pineapple grown on English soil, but at the time such a feat was an impossibility, for hothouses, or heated glasshouses, to keep the plants sufficiently warm during our cold winters, had yet to be invented. The painting probably commemorates the first pineapples *ripened* in one of the King's gardens from an imported, already-growing plant.

The great European pineapple-growing race was not actually won until the following decade, and William III, who came to Britain to reign with his wife Mary in 1689, was the proud ruler of the victorious kingdom; one of his Dutch subjects, a woman named Agneta Block, had successfully grown a pineapple from seed on her estate near Leiden in 1687. Naturally, it being a symbol of both prosperity and gardening skill, the plant-mad royal couple had the pineapple among their envied collection of exotics, but their gardeners never succeeded in growing one from scratch in Britain. It was not until some years after both their deaths that a pineapple was home-grown, in a non-royal garden in Richmond.

The achievement kick-started an 18th-century craze for the fruit, though few Britons of the era would ever get close to a real pineapple. They were enormously costly to cultivate in a dedicated hothouse, even more so than oranges or grapes. Estimates suggest that around the time George III came to the throne in the 1760s, the total cost of producing a single pineapple averaged about £80 – much more than an aristocrat paid their butler for an entire year's work, so if not solely accessible to those with a royally large income, then near enough. Even if you were invited to dine in an enormously wealthy household in George's reign, you were more likely to be sitting and looking at a pineapple, placed with great pride on the table, than actually sampling it.

George III and his wife Charlotte had a 'pinery' at both Kew and Hampton Court, and Royal Gardener Lancelot 'Capability' Brown had his salary topped up with an extra £100 a year for growing pineapples for them, reflecting the time and elaborate care required. They could better afford to indulge than their subjects, with a pineapple on the table on Christmas Day, and a 'profusion' of them supplied for a banquet at Windsor Castle. Pineapples also featured on the menu in the residence of their notoriously gluttonous son, the future George IV, who even enjoyed the luxury of pineapple jelly.

ABOVE
Charles II is presented with a pineapple, probably the first successfully ripened in one of his gardens. 'Charles II Presented with a Pineapple' by Hendrick Danckerts, c. 1675-80.

The pineapple had lost little of its glamour and none of its air of affluence by the time of George IV's lavish coronation in 1821, a full 160 years after Charles II first beheld one. A remarkably large 11-lb specimen was the crowning glory of the banquet of similarly colossal proportions held at Westminster Hall after the ceremony – not just the king of fruits, but the king of the table.

In recent years appropriate consideration has been given to the pineapple as a symbol of Britain's far-reaching colonialist power and the slave trade that operated out of, among other places, Barbados – a timely reminder of the juxtaposition between the pineapple's regal status among fruit, and its complicated place within our history.

OPPOSITE
A silver side table featuring a life-size pineapple, commissioned by William III for Kensington Palace in 1698.

ABOVE
The grand feast depicted in 'Coronation Banquet of George IV in Westminster Hall', 1821.

RIGHT
'Royalty in a Rage or Family Quarrels', a cartoon by Robert Cruikshank lampooning the notoriously gluttonous George IV, 1820. A pineapple has pride of place on the table behind.

way
Hollo Georgy mind what you'r after if you offend Fred: he has got a Red Rod in Pickle for you"
Hell and Torment – what! my own Family all against me – there then take that, and that
Bravo Bravo George! dont spare them an Inch – For 20 Ducats you can obtain ye Affidavit of any Servant in Italy or I'm not Cunning
Pub.d July 23 1820 by King Chancery Lane
or Family Quarrels –
Suppressed

CARPINUS

HORNBEAM

The hornbeam tree and its pretty, pleated foliage holds a special place in the history of Hampton Court Palace; it was used to create the famous hedge maze, the world's oldest surviving example.

IN THE MEANDERING PATHS and confounding corners of this venerable maze, thought to have been commissioned around 1690 for joint sovereigns William III and Mary II, plants collided with the leisurely royal pursuit of pleasure, and were grown and trained purely to test, delight and divert those who had the privilege to wander their grounds.

Hornbeam was a practical choice for the maze's hedges, being, as one 19th-century garden writer put it, 'extremely patient of the knife' and offering dense, if not evergreen, foliage. But the maze's curious trapezoidal shape, which covers a third of an acre, had to be dictated by the layout of the 'wilderness' area in which it was created – contrary to its name, this was a formal, almost geometrical garden. Its series of 'rooms' separated by high, clipped hedges, also of hornbeam, offered spaces for peaceful retreat, private assignations and entertaining surprises, the maze being one of the latter.

It was neither the first of its kind in Britain, nor the first royal hedge maze. Labyrinths with walls tall enough for a person to be lost from sight began to appear towards the end of the 16th century. There was one at Nonsuch – Henry VIII's palace in Surrey – which by 1599 was sufficiently well-grown that 'one could neither go over or through' it. There was also one at Theobalds, the house James I persuaded Lord

OPPOSITE
Hampton Court Palace's world-famous hedge maze.

Burghley to swap for the royal residence of Hatfield. But neither house, let alone its maze, survives today.

It is somewhat surprising that the one at Hampton Court does. Mazes had fallen out of fashion by the time that Lancelot 'Capability' Brown – who firmly favoured sweeping, natural vistas over contrived baroque scenes – became Master Gardener at Hampton Court in 1764. He had torn out several mazes in his illustrious career as the nation's pre-eminent country-house landscaper, but was given strict instructions by King George III not to interfere with the hornbeam. So, as the palace's formal gardens dwindled into decline around it, Brown having reportedly 'declined the hopeless task' of improving them, the maze remained rooted.

When the gates of the palace were flung open to visitors in 1838, it was no longer privileged courtiers but the great British public who took up the maze's challenge. Somewhere in the region of ten million visitors lost themselves in its thickets before Queen Victoria's reign was over. And while the versatile hornbeam derives its name from the strength of its timber – its wood being likened to horn – it is hardly surprising that by the 20th century, after two hundred years in situ and more explorers careering to the maze's centre than William, Mary or their gardeners could ever have imagined, the hedges had taken a battering. The maze had to be renewed several times. Although the majority of the current hedge is formed of robust and evergreen yew, in the mid-2010s the centre of the maze was planted with hornbeam, bringing the story of the iconic maze, after a few twists and turns, back to its royal beginnings.

ABOVE
The maze's hedges were replanted with yew in the 20th century, but the palace gardeners have re-introduced the original hornbeam to the centre.

ST.HIL. PL. FRANCE.

CHARDON MARIE.

Cirsium

Thistle

Theories abound as to exactly why, how and when the prickly thistle with its striking purple crown became the proud emblem of Scotland.

Some say the distinctive flower (or weed, depending on your sympathies) was adopted because its spear-shaped leaves resembled those the fierce and fearless Scots massed against their enemy in battle. Others, that it dates to the Middle Ages, and an attempt by a Norse army to ambush the Scots with a silent, barefooted invasion – a plan that was thwarted when they stepped into a field of thistles, their shrieks raising the alarm and resulting in their resounding defeat. Yet another theory proposes that the House of Stuart, Scotland's reigning dynasty from 1371 until 1714, copied the thistle emblem from their French allies.

Whether the last has any truth or not, there is no denying that royals have contributed to its emblematic status. In the reign of James III in the 15th century, Scottish coins began to bear the thistle motif, and the plant appeared behind portraits of the King and his wife on a contemporary altarpiece.

By the time his son James IV married the English princess Margaret Tudor (Henry VIII's sister) in 1503, it was firmly entwined with both the Scottish crown and the nation as a whole. Thistles trailed the illuminated borders of the official documentation of their union, and new windows were fitted in the Palace of Holyroodhouse, where the wedding took place, interlacing the Scottish thistle with the English rose.

OPPOSITE
The thistle, proud emblem of Scotland; illustration from the Natural History Museum Collection.

The hardy thistle was also incorporated into the Great Seal of Scotland by the couple's equally resilient daughter Mary, Queen of Scots. Thistles still grow abundantly on the small mound that is all that remains of Fotheringhay Castle in Northamptonshire, where she was executed on the reluctant order of Elizabeth I in 1587; a slice of Scotland sprung from seeds believed to have been scattered by Mary herself or her attendants.

Mary's son and heir James VI of Scotland inherited the English throne on the death of Elizabeth in 1603, and it was he who brought the thistle into its heraldry. Famously keen to promote what he called the 'blessed union' of the two countries and crowns, he took for his badge a somewhat awkward combination of the English and Scottish emblems, splicing together, or dimidiating, half a thistle and half a rose. It was a symbol that would be adopted by all his male successors.

The thistle embedded itself into royal ceremonial life even further when James VII and II formally established the Order of the Thistle in 1687, a Scottish order of chivalry equivalent to the English Order of the Garter, with a motto that deliberately puns on its country's spiky emblem, '*Nemo me impune lacessit*' – 'no one provokes me with impunity'. Every other year, the sovereign and members of the Order still don their green velvet robes and glittering collars for a procession into Edinburgh's St Giles' Cathedral for the Order of the Thistle Service.

King George IV once processed through the same city's streets, during his historic visit to Scotland in 1822 – the first time a reigning British monarch had ventured north of the English border in over 150 years. In doing so, however, he may have caused the confusion that lingers over which variety is the 'true' Scottish thistle. Sir Walter Scott, who choreographed much of the King's trip, chose *Onopordum acanthium* – the non-native and comparatively rare 'cotton thistle' – to be carried in the various processions, rather than *Cirsium vulgare*, the native 'spear thistle' that the first Stuart Kings would have seen growing abundantly across their highlands and islands. The inhospitable thistle had caught them both out in a case of show over substance, but then our most extravagant monarch probably didn't mind that.

ABOVE
In adulthood, James VI and I united the Scottish and English thrones and brought thistles and roses together in heraldry. This illustration was first published in *Memoirs of the Court of Queen Elizabeth*, 1825.

ABOVE
Like the rose and the shamrock, the thistle features on the uniform of the Tower of London's Yeoman Warders.

ABOVE
A fragment from Queen Victoria's coronation robe, incorporating the Scottish national flower.

Citrus × sinensis

Orange tree

The orange tree is associated with Britain's only joint sovereigns, William and Mary. It was also the mainstay of Mary's envy-inducing collection of exotic plants and flowers.

The couple, both keen horticulturalists, were invited to take the throne in 1689, after the inadvisable attempt by Mary's father King James II to Catholicise his new kingdom resulted in his forced exile and abdication. Mary's was the real claim to the crown, but William, Prince of Orange and ruler of the Netherlands, had been prepared to accept nothing less than a joint monarchy, under which he shared equal power and status with his wife. They had never been an obvious match – Mary was twelve years younger, high-spirited and nearly six feet tall; William was short, humourless and in indifferent health – but by the time Mary returned to her childhood home as Queen, they were a strong and devoted couple, united especially by their shared passion for plants and gardens.

In their new grounds at Hampton Court, they were keen to make their mark on the landscape. As Daniel Defoe put it, under their stewardship, the palace gardens 'put on new cloaths and [were] dress'd gay and glorious'. They were soon also home to around 1,000 orange trees of different, sometimes rare, varieties, carried over from the couple's residences in Holland. Not only were these trees a tangible symbol of the origins of the new King and his Dutch realm, but a powerful statement of the couple's wealth and fashionable taste. Orange trees would have been wildly

OPPOSITE
Joint sovereigns William III and Mary II. William was also the Prince of Orange. 'Portrait of Willem II, Prince of Orange, and his Wife Mary Stuart' by Gerard van Honthorst, 1647.

unattainable for the vast majority of their subjects. They were expensive to buy – costing almost £1 10s (around £250 today) each compared to pear trees at sixpence a time. And they were even more expensive and labour-intensive to cultivate, requiring glasshouses or orangeries to shelter them from the worst of Britain's weather in the winter months.

The couple had both built at the palace for this very purpose, along with 'stoves' or hot houses where their other plants could be given the warmer temperatures they needed to flourish. For the orange trees made up just half of a wider collection of 2,000 exotic species, gathered from the far reaches of the globe for the 'plantaholic' Queen by the Dutch East India Company, as well as by specially commissioned plant hunters. It was one of the largest private collections of plants in the world, greatly admired and envied. Under Mary's direction, Hampton Court became home to all sorts of tender species previously unseen in her home city, from cacti to bananas, and jasmine to geraniums. All were carefully nurtured by her own personal botanist, Dr Leonard Plukenet.

In the summer months, the royal gardeners would have the back-breaking task of moving the couple's orange trees, along with these exotics, out into the garden in elaborate pots. There, they could serve their primary purpose of impressing the Queen's visitors. The fruits they produced would have been too bitter for any of her guests to eat raw, but some may have tasted them at the royal table, for Mary had them harvested to make marmalade.

Mary and her husband were not the first royals to have a fondness for oranges. Henry VIII, however, had to have his imported from Spain at great cost. The purchase of an orange strainer for his household in 1534 is a sign of the frequency with which exotic citrus flavours and preserves were appearing on his plate in the period. Royal cooks were also able to make use of the fragrant white blossom of the orange tree, adding orange flower water to various dishes.

The pretty blossom had more special significance to another royal couple – one who shared the throne in spirit, if not like William and Mary in statute, Victoria and Albert. The cousins became engaged while the Prince Consort was on his second visit to London in October 1839; Victoria proposed just five days after his arrival. While the engagement

LEFT AND BELOW
Oranges growing at Hampton Court Palace. The pots with green bands are replicas of those purchased for William and Mary.

ABOVE
A portrait of Queen Victoria in her bridal attire, painted for Prince Albert to mark their seventh wedding anniversary, by Franz Xaver Winterhalter, 1847.

was to be as short as possible, there was no avoiding Albert returning to his native Coburg to arrange his affairs, ready for his move to Britain, and one of the first gifts he sent back to his fiancée was a delicate gold and porcelain brooch in the form of a sprig of orange blossom. 'May you think with love of your faithful Albert when you take it into your hand,' the accompanying note read, sending his waiting bride into raptures.

With their pure white petals, orange flowers were, naturally, an emblem of chastity in the 'language of flowers' that had captured the Victorian imagination. That being so, it was already a popular choice for wedding gowns and headdresses, but it's tempting to think that Albert's romantic gift had some influence on Victoria's enthusiastic trimming of her bridal attire with orange blossom; from the simple, strikingly unmajestic wreath she wore on her head to the posy on her bodice, it featured prominently. And it set the fashion for scores of brides who followed, both royal and otherwise. Among them were Victoria's daughter-in-law, the future Queen Alexandra, who chose a wide headdress of artificial orange blossom in 1863, and her daughter-in-law, the future Queen Mary, whose bodice and skirt were heavily garnished with trails of orange flowers thirty years later.

For Victoria and Albert, the blossom certainly remained a bloom emblematic of their love for each other; by 1846, Albert had gifted a delighted Victoria several additional pieces to match the original brooch, including earrings, and a wreath for her hair that she particularly treasured. On every one of the twenty-one wedding anniversaries they celebrated together, she wore parts of the set. Even in her widowhood, when the jewellery, with all its memories, was presumably too painful to wear, the Queen's connection with the flower continued; one of her granddaughters recalled that she wore 'a faint perfume of orange blossom', a scent that was made for her in the French city of Grasse, fragrance capital of the world. And on her death in 1901, the Queen left a firm instruction: the orange blossom set was not to be passed on to any of her children, but instead placed in the Blue Room at Windsor Castle, maintained as a shrine to her beloved husband since his death forty years before hers.

ABOVE
The four pieces of orange blossom jewellery gifted to Queen Victoria by Prince Albert between 1839 and 1846.

ABOVE
Princess Mary of Teck and the future King George V on their wedding day in July 1893.

Convallaria Majalis

Lily of the Valley

As Britain's two longest-reigning monarchs, both beloved and mourned deeply after their deaths, Queen Victoria and Elizabeth II have much in common, but they also share a favourite flower: the fragrant lily of the valley.

Though she adored most spring blooms, the lily of the valley was Victoria's favourite from early childhood, as she confided in her journal. There, she also recorded the countless occasions when her children and, later, grandchildren greeted her with posies of the tiny flowers on the morning of her birthday. They were a particularly apt gift for a May-born Queen, since lily of the valley, which blooms in the spring, is the month's birth flower, and is sometimes known as 'May Bells' or 'May Lilly'.

The late Queen Elizabeth, meanwhile, revealed that lily of the valley was her own favourite flower in 2020, ahead of that year's virtual Chelsea Flower Show, which, as patron of Britain's Royal Horticultural Society, she had rarely missed in the decades before. It was also a great favourite of her mother (who picked great bunches of it for her childhood bedroom at Glamis Castle). Lily of the valley featured in the Queen's bridal bouquet when she married Prince Philip in 1947, just as it has done in many other royal bridal bouquets since, including those of Queen Camilla, Catherine, Princess of Wales, and Meghan, Duchess of Sussex. It had also been included in her late Majesty's coronation bouquet in 1953, and, partly in tribute, it appeared on Queen Camilla's velvet Robe of Estate at the coronation in 2023.

OPPOSITE
The dainty bridal bouquet of Catherine, Princess of Wales combined lily of the valley with sweet william, hyacinth and myrtle.

In fact, the flower's royal favour stretches back much further than either Queen Victoria or Elizabeth II; it can be traced back to 16th-century France, and a posy presented to King Charles IX on May Day as a good luck charm. He turned the gift into a tradition, presenting bouquets of '*le muguet*' to the ladies of his court every year on 1 May, and to this day the French do the same, buying and exchanging lilies of the valley for luck on what is known as *La Fête du Muguet*.

It is, however, an interesting choice for a royal favourite. For while lily of the valley looks the very picture of innocence with its snow-white, bell-shaped blooms, which nod regally in the breeze, the whole plant is highly toxic, for both humans and animals. According to an exhibitor at Chelsea in 2016, who reminded her late Majesty of the plant's poisonous potential, the Queen reportedly responded, with her trademark dry wit, 'I've been given two bunches this week. Perhaps they want me dead.' Its sweet, gentle scent and delicate, bell-shaped flowers, however, made the lily of the valley perfect for nosegays of the sort presented to Queens past and present, despite its dark side.

The flower has been a staple of the royal gardens, too, growing profusely at both Sandringham and Buckingham Palace. One afternoon in the late 1970s, Prime Minister James Callaghan returned to Downing Street with a sprig in his buttonhole, picked and placed there by the late Queen as they conducted their weekly audience on a stroll around her London garden. It's hard to imagine Queen Victoria doing the same, though she was known to send bouquets of spring flowers to the favourite among her own prime ministers, Benjamin Disraeli.

OPPOSITE
Elizabeth II leaves Buckingham Palace for her coronation in 1953; her bouquet included her favourite flower, lily of the valley.

ABOVE
Queen Victoria's third son, Prince Arthur, holds a sprig of their shared birth flower in a painting from May 1851. 'The First of May' by Franz Xaver Winterhalter.

ABOVE
The late Queen was frequently given posies of the delicate and sweetly scented bloom.

HAGTORN, CRATÆGUS OXYACANTHA L.

CRATAEGUS

HAWTHORN

Every December, Britain's monarch receives a cutting from a very special hawthorn tree, and uses it to decorate their Christmas table.

THE SOVEREIGN'S SPRIG COMES FROM A TREE in the Somerset town of Glastonbury. Unlike most of our common hedgerow hawthorns, which blossom annually around May (and are often known as 'May Trees'), the Glastonbury thorn is a descendant of an unusual variety that flowers twice a year, offering a lavish showing of its highly scented snowy-white blossom once around Easter time, and once around Christmas. With no apparent horticultural precedent for its second winter blooms, there has been space for a legend to grow around it over the centuries. The tree, the story went, was a miracle of God, the result of a visit from Saint Joseph of Arimathea, who, having travelled to Britain to spread the message of Christianity, drove his staff into the ground on Glastonbury's Wearyall Hill, where it took root and flowered.

The tradition of sending a budded branch of this 'holy thorn' to the monarch as a seasonal gift is not, however, a very old one. It dates back only to 1929, when the vicar of the parish, a staunch champion of Glastonbury and its many myths and legends, learned that on at least one occasion twigs from its legendary thorn were presented to Anne of Denmark, the wife of James I, and so decided to despatch

OPPOSITE
Illustration of the hawthorn tree from Carl Lindman's *Bilder ur Nordens Flora*, 1905.

one to the Royal Palace for Queen Mary. Over the ensuing years it became the custom, shortly before Christmas, to hold a ceremony in the grounds of St John's Church, home of a tree descended from the original on Wearyall Hill, to take the cutting that would be sent to the Queen, and in later years to both Queen Elizabeth II and the Queen Mother.

The late Queen was said to use the sprig to decorate her dining table on Christmas Day. Clearly she did not find the hawthorn blossom's heavy and very distinctive scent, likened over the centuries to the smell of plague or death, too repulsive. The King reportedly also has a hawthorn grown from the one at Glastonbury in his own garden at Highgrove.

The connection between the 'holy' thorn of Glastonbury and the monarch may be comparatively recent, but hawthorn itself was, in fact, entwined with the royal story much earlier. Legend has it that as the bloody Battle of Bosworth drew to a close in 1485, ending the life and reign of Richard III and the Wars of the Roses, the victor, Henry Tudor, was given Richard's crown, which had been found by one of his men hanging in a hawthorn bush. It may be just one of many myths about the battle, though the new King Henry VII was quick to adopt a crowned hawthorn as one of his heraldic emblems, putting it to profitable use as propaganda.

His son Henry VIII, meanwhile, was one of many Tudors for whom the annual hawthorn blossom was a sight not to be missed. Like many of his subjects he was known to go 'a-maying' – to venture into the woods and perhaps bring home for himself some of the sprigs that are now delivered to the door of his modern-day successors.

OPPOSITE TOP
Queen Elizabeth II receiving the holy thorn.

OPPOSITE BOTTOM
The hawthorn tree in the grounds of St John's Church in Glastonbury supplies the sovereign's Christmas sprig.

A Glastonbury
Holy Thorn

Delphinium Elatum

Delphinium

It's no secret that the showy, stately delphinium, a majestic presence in any summer border, is the favourite flower of the most green-fingered king in our history.

'I have an absolute passion for delphiniums – and I've always had it,' King Charles has said of the bloom which, as he puts it, 'holds pride of place in my botanical affections'.

Such is his enthusiasm for the flowers that he has been patron of The Delphinium Society since 2018, and delphiniums grow in abundance nearly everywhere he has a garden; from Birkhall, the house on the edge of the Balmoral estate in Royal Deeside, which he inherited from his grandmother, to the gardens at Sandringham in Norfolk, which have had a refresh since he came to the throne. It is at Highgrove House in the Cotswolds that they are at their most conspicuous, however, especially in the Sundial Garden, where banks of their tall and majestic spires in exceptionally pretty blues, pinks and purples make a statement in the summer months.

Charles is affectionately referred to as 'The Boss' by his gardening team at Highgrove, but the King is no mere supervisor, rather he's a hands-on gardener, ready to don his wellingtons and get digging, crediting gardening with keeping him sane. (He is always keen to get stuck in with the hard, physical work of hedge-laying, too, which he quips usually

OPPOSITE
The late Queen Mother is said to have influenced the garden tastes of her grandson Charles.

makes him look as if he has 'just come off the field at Agincourt'.) Yet, before purchasing Highgrove in 1980, he 'knew nothing about the practical aspects of gardening', as he modestly reminds those daunted by the scale of his achievements there.

Gardening is in the King's blood, however. Both of his maternal grandparents, George VI and Queen Elizabeth, were passionate about plants and hands-on in their gardens. One of the Highgrove gardening team has credited the late Queen Mother with a particular influence on her grandson's garden tastes, in terms of colour and scent. They were certainly very close right up until her death in 2002, and Charles has said that she was wonderfully encouraging of his efforts. The Stumpery at Highgrove contains one of his memorials to her; the bronze relief at the centre of the Temple of Worthies shows her in her felt gardening hat and pearls, watching over his creation as it grows and changes. Delphiniums – especially blue ones – were flowers she liked, too, and she supervised the planting of a dedicated border to them at Buckingham Palace during her time in residence, decades before her grandson scattered the stately blooms across all his royal gardens.

ABOVE
Pink and blue delphiniums in the Sundial Garden at Highgrove House.

HER MAJESTY QUEEN ELIZABETH.
LP.3

DIANTHUS CARYOPHYLLUS

CARNATION

The carnation was known to the Greeks and Romans who used it to create ceremonial crowns, and it is from this association with 'coronations' that some say one of the oldest flowers to adorn our gardens derived its name.

WHETHER TRUTH OR JUST AN APPEALING TALE, the carnation does have a long royal history to match its regal sounding moniker. Though it's arrival on these shores can't be traced accurately, by the time of the Tudors, carnations – then more usually known as 'gillyflowers' or 'gilloflowers' – were firm favourites. The flowers that are often dismissed as commonplace and old-fashioned today, were soon to become – as botanist John Parkinson declared them in 1629 – 'the chiefest flowers of account in all our English gardens', admired for combining a hardiness necessary for our climate with a delicate scent.

The bloom had acquired a strong association with love and marriage, which meant it made regular appearances in betrothal or marriage portraits of the era – including royal ones. The image of Prince Arthur, older brother of Henry VIII, holding a white carnation was probably created to mark his engagement to Katherine of Aragon in the late 1490s. There is also a carnation in the earliest known full-length depiction of Elizabeth I. The 'Hampden Portrait', created around 1563, shows the young(ish) Queen – she was then about thirty years of age – against a background of fruits and flowers, and clasping in her hand a single red carnation, all of which proclaimed her potential as a marriage partner and a mother.

OPPOSITE
A glamorous young Queen Elizabeth II holds a large bouquet of carnations and roses.

Dianthus ferrugineus.

Miss Mintern del.

OPPOSITE
Illustration of a yellow carnation by Augusta Withers, Flower Painter in Ordinary to Queen Adelaide.

ABOVE
Queen Elizabeth I clasps a single carnation in the 'Hampden Portrait', possibly painted to attract suitors. By Steven Van Der Meulen, c. 1563.

The Tudor term 'gillyflower' is generally agreed to have been a catch-all term for various forms of the *Dianthus*, including both the carnation and its very close relative the 'pink' – both of which have enjoyed royal favour. Henrietta Maria, the unpopular Catholic consort of Charles I, reputedly grew numerous pinks, and may even have introduced a number of varieties from her native France – that is, before the outbreak of the English Civil War and her husband's subsequent execution forced her to flee back to her homeland.

Meanwhile, one of her much later successors, Queen Adelaide, had a 'very tasteful' collection of carnations in her flower garden at Windsor Castle in the early 19th century, according to London nurseryman Thomas Hogg, one of her suppliers. The wife of William IV, Adelaide had been hastily picked as his bride in 1818, amid the scramble to produce an heir to the throne after the death of George III's only legitimate grandchild. Unlike her ill-fated predecessor, she was so well respected that well over a dozen varieties of the flower she was so particularly fond of were named in her honour.

Adelaide's collection perhaps contributed to the carnation's status as a flower of fashion (though some cynics put it down to the fact that unlike so many other flowers, they bloomed in late summer, when the wealthy and titled were returning to the comparative dullness of their country seats after the end of the London season). Adelaide helped to further encourage interest in carnations, along with blooms such as tulips and auriculas, by becoming a patron of some of the 'floricultural' societies that were springing up around the country.

King Edward VII's garden at Sandringham was similarly famed for its display of carnations at the start of the following century, but his were not simply for show. Carnations were a bloom of choice for buttonholes, the flowers pinned to the lapel of any self-respecting Edwardian man of fashion, and the gardens had to provide a steady supply for the King.

OPPOSITE
A selection of carnations by botanical illustrator Augusta Withers, whose royal patron had numerous varieties named in her honour, 1857.

4

2

3

6

5

1

TREE CARNATION.

Mrs Withers, Delt.

Printed by C. Chabot.

1. Ariadne.
2. Beauty.
3. Garibaldi.
4. Perfection.
5. Queen of Whites.
6. Queen of Yellows.

ILLUSTRATED BOUQUET.

Published by E. G. Henderson and Son.

OPPOSITE
Queen Adelaide, the wife of King William IV, painted by Sir William Beechey, c. 1831.

ABOVE
Queen Elizabeth II is presented with a bouquet containing carnations while at Sandringham Flower Show, 1984.

ÄLGGRÄS, SPIRÆA ULMARIA L.

Gen. Stab. Lit. Anst.

Filipendula Ulmaria

Meadowsweet

'Queen Elizabeth of famous memory did more desire it than any other sweet herbe to strew her chambers', it was said of the fragrant, frothy-flowering meadowsweet.

A plant sacred to the Druids, meadowsweet's earliest practical use was as a flavouring for soups, wines and beers, as reflected in its name, which derives from the Anglo-Saxon '*meodu-swete*', meaning 'mead-sweetener'. But it was thanks to its heady, almost sickly-sweet scent – which 'makes the heart merrie and joyful and delighteth the senses', according to 16th-century herbalist John Gerard – that meadowsweet was in demand at the Elizabethan court, to strew over the floors to mask the many unpleasant smells that permeated even the most luxuriously appointed royal palaces, particularly as a result of poor sanitation.

Elizabeth I was known to be acutely sensitive to all such unsavoury odours, so rushes, herbs and flowers would be generously scattered over the floors of the most-used chambers and parlours of her residences, and then periodically swept up and replaced with fresh ones. The practice was not confined to the royal palaces: Elizabeth's courtier – and 'favourite' – Robert Dudley spent £1 7s 9d on various strewing herbs in 1558, the equivalent of about £700 today. Nor did strewing only keep undesirable smells at bay. It also helped to deter vermin and repel insects (the more bitter tansy, now known to contain a natural insecticide, was another herb much used by the Tudors for the latter purpose).

OPPOSITE
Illustration of meadowsweet from Carl Lindman's *Bilder ur Nordens Flora*, 1905.

What made the aromatic leaves of meadowsweet 'farre excelle' all other strewing herbs was, as Gerard put it, that 'neither doth it cause headache, or lothsomnesse to meat, as some other sweete smelling herbs do' – which perhaps explains why it enjoyed particular favour with Queen Elizabeth, who was known to be plagued by headaches.

Not all of Elizabeth's subjects would have been so keen to strew the plant's creamy-white, foaming blooms inside their house with abandon, for it was considered deeply unlucky by some. If a person was to fall asleep with meadowsweet in the room it was said they might not wake up. And hay-fever sufferers would certainly find it less than delightful to their senses, for the fluffy petals that proliferate between June and September fall easily enough even when they are not being tossed about the floor, sending pollen dust everywhere.

But Elizabeth was clearly neither a sufferer nor superstitious. She appears not to have had an official 'herb strewer' on the payroll to scatter her meadowsweet for her; instead, the task probably fell to one of her ladies or household staff. Later sovereigns, from Charles II onwards, did employ a Herb Strewer, however, and the position remained until the death of the last incumbent, one Mary Rayner, who lived long enough to serve William IV in the 1830s.

Yet though her predecessors had been called upon to scatter herbs at coronations from James II's onwards, Mary Rayner was denied the opportunity to showcase her skills at the most extravagant and expensive in history – and the last to feature a herb strewer – the coronation of George IV in 1821. Instead, an old acquaintance of the King's, Miss Anne Fellowes, became 'Herb Woman' for the day. Accompanied by several aristocratic 'maids' and dressed in a scarlet mantle, she led the Coronation Procession between Westminster Hall and the Abbey, showering flowers and fragrant herbs from a small hand basket, playing at a part that had once served a very practical purpose at the Elizabethan court some 250 years before.

OPPOSITE
The 16th-century herbalist John Gerard, drawn by William Rogers, taken from Gerard's book *The Herball or Generall Historie of Plantes*, 1597.

EFFIGIES IOANNIS GERAR
CESTRESHYRII CIVIS ET CHIRVR-
GI LONDINENSIS ANNO Æ
TATIS SVÆ 53 1598.

OPPOSITE
Sweet-smelling herbs are scattered at the coronation of James II in 1685. From Francis Sandford's 'The History of the Coronation of ... James II', 1687.

stm.r
The high Constable of Westminster.
A Fife.
4 Drums.
The Drum Major.
(5)

A. SMULTRON, FRAGARIA VESCA L.

B. BACKSMULTRON, FRAGARIA VIRIDIS DUCH.

FRAGARIA × ANANASSA

STRAWBERRY

Not just delicious summer fruits, strawberries are a failsafe crop for beginners, which is perhaps why they were cultivated by Queen Victoria's children at their beloved holiday home, Osborne House, on the Isle of Wight.

'BERTIE', THE FUTURE EDWARD VII, his five sisters and three brothers all had the luxury of a sizeable plot of their own at Osborne in which to discover the delights of gardening. Situated near the Swiss Cottage, the Alpine-style chalet built for them to play at keeping house, each of their gardens was big enough to accommodate fourteen beds. Two of them were for strawberries, a favourite with royals for centuries, notably Henry VIII and Anne Boleyn. James I, meanwhile, enjoyed the sweet and juicy fruits so much, a courtier recalled, that whenever freshly picked strawberries and cherries were presented to him, 'his hand was in the basket' before his servant even had time to announce them with a speech.

The Saxe-Coburg children had two more beds for gooseberries, two for currants, two for raspberries and two for various flowers, with the remainder set aside for growing an array of vegetables, including asparagus and artichokes. Each prince and princess also had their own scaled-down set of tools, with every hoe, rake, spade and wheelbarrow monogrammed with the initials of their royal owner, and kept in a dedicated tool house.

The produce they planted and nurtured was assessed by Osborne's under-gardener, and if it was of sufficient quality, Prince Albert, who viewed the garden as an immensely

OPPOSITE
Illustration taken from Carl Lindman's *Bilder ur Nordens Flora (Pictures of Northern Flora)*, 1905.

important educational tool, would pay the child who had grown it the market rate. It seems likely that the children, who were also taught to bake in the Swiss Cottage kitchen, used, and consumed, the fruits of their labours, too.

They were neither the first royal children to be given space to grow, nor the last. King George III had developed his fascination with agriculture (which earned him the nickname 'Farmer George') through his own childhood garden, and in the 1770s Bertie's maternal grandfather and his brothers had been given small plots of their own at Kew, the family's country residence, which they were expected to cultivate. They sowed them with wheat, which they too 'weeded, reaped and harvested … solely by themselves' before making it into bread for their parents' table. Victoria's children seem to have relished their outdoor play – Princess Beatrice, in particular, carried on gardening into adulthood – but in the case of the Georgian princes, the enforced experience, intended to similarly ground their royal feet in aspects of ordinary life, singularly failed to give them green fingers.

King George VI must have enjoyed his early experiences of growing vegetables on an allotment at Frogmore House far more, for he ensured that his two daughters, Elizabeth and Margaret Rose, had their own gardens at Royal Lodge, Windsor. Before the Second World War, their patch was pretty rather than practical; a display of blooms including hydrangeas, aubretias and baby azaleas. But after war broke out in 1939, the two princesses joined in the nationwide 'Dig for Victory' campaign. The flowerbeds on Windsor Castle's East Terrace were all turned over to vegetables, and two small plots were theirs. They grew tomatoes, sweetcorn and beans – and posed for photographs, their planting having turned from mere childhood play into part of their royal role.

ABOVE
Princesses Elizabeth and Margaret Rose digging for victory in the grounds of Windsor Castle in 1943.

OPPOSITE
Prince Albert, consort of Queen Victoria. He encouraged their children to grow fruit and vegetables. By William Drummond, c. 1841.

ABOVE
The Swiss Cottage at Osborne House; the royal children each had their own plot in its garden. Drawn by William Leighton Leitch in 1855.

N2031.

Pub. by S. Curtis. Walworth. Dec. 1. 1818. Weddell. Sc.

Gentiana

Gentian

The vibrant gentian flower was used as a medicinal treatment for King George III during his mental illness, and may have been responsible for his most famous symptom.

The 'pale blue ring' spotted by those keeping a close eye on the colour of the King's urine has become legendary, but it was just one of a very long list of disturbing symptoms displayed by the monarch during the four prolonged periods of illness he suffered during the latter half of his life.

His first major attack came in 1788, when he was recorded as delusional, swearing and shouting, talking for nineteen hours with scarcely a pause and attempting sexual assaults, as well as suffering terrifying convulsions, swollen legs and feet, and all sorts of aches and pains. Unable to disguise his mania, a decision was made to confine him in his house, close to what is now named Kew Palace, for treatment. There, he made a recovery within months, but there were two further relapses, each more severe than the last, and by 1810 the King had succumbed to a combination of chronic mania and dementia. He spent the rest of his life in seclusion at Windsor, a stranger even to his own family.

George's oddly coloured urine was one of the key symptoms used to support a hypothetical diagnosis of his malady as the genetic blood disorder, porphyria, first made by two psychiatrists in the 1960s. But it now appears that the use of gentian flowers in the medicinal war chest of the King's multiple doctors may actually be to blame.

The flower aptly takes its name from another king, Gentius, of the ancient kingdom of Illyria, who was reputedly the

OPPOSITE
Blue gentian flowers were used in the treatment of George III; unknown artist, 1819.

first to discover its medicinal qualities, and which has been used as a tonic for digestive problems for thousands of years. Seventeenth-century herbalists recommended it to 'easeth pains in the stomach', which were among the things complained of by the ailing King. When his most alarming symptom appeared, it was just three days after he was given extract of gentian, which is known to turn the urine a bluey-purple colour thanks to the intensity of its deep-blue blooms. They are, indeed, so vibrant that they have been used in the making of blue dyes. With many more mentions in George's medical notes of 'pale' or 'clear' urine, the impact of the gentian begins to look like the most logical explanation for the apparently troubling symptom.

For many more reasons, porphyria is largely regarded as a modern misdiagnosis of George's condition, but it remains difficult to settle on a firm alternative, since the accounts of his illness differ wildly and are now nearly 250 years old. And with the Prince of Wales so very eager to step up to the throne as Regent, the reports of the doctors he installed in his father's household to advise on his fitness to rule cannot be entirely trusted.

But with doubt thrown on a medical reason for his famous blue urine, a new theory has emerged: that George was, as his subjects always suspected, suffering from a psychiatric illness. Quite possibly bipolar disorder, a diagnosis that fits better with the changes in his writing and speech patterns, his tendency to talk himself hoarse, and the fact that his bouts of ill-health coincided with periods of great stress in his life. The pretty gentian flower may just have helped to throw everyone off the scent.

OPPOSITE
A 19th-century illustration of gentian flowers in bloom by Pierre-Joseph Redouté.

Gentiane sans tige. *Gentianæ acaulis.*

ABOVE
Kew Palace, where King George III was confined during two of his later episodes of ill health.

OPPOSITE
George III in his later years, by William Beechey, c. 1800. Between 1811 and his death in 1820, he was permanently confined at Windsor Castle.

1cm
JG

Lavandula

Lavender

'Lavender's blue, dilly dilly, Lavender's green, when I am King, dilly dilly, you shall be Queen' goes the famous rhyme, but does it tell a royal tale?

If it did refer to any Queen, the most likely candidate would be Henrietta Maria, daughter of the French monarch, whose marriage with the ill-fated Charles I was arranged in the months before he ascended to the throne in 1625. At the house her new husband purchased for her at Wimbledon, she is known to have overseen the creation of a fine and much admired garden, complete with 'great and large borders' of lavender, one of her favourites plants, especially the now-rare white variety.

Yet evidence to link her – or any of our other Queens – to the rhyme is scant. The argument that the 17th-century folk song has its origins in the choosing of a king and queen for the festivities of Twelfth Night – the last day of the Christmas season, then marked by much feasting and general mischief-making, all overseen by the acting royals – seems entirely credible. Not least because in its earliest versions the song's lyrics were distinctly on the bawdy side.

Nonetheless, the aromatic lavender, with its attractive profusion of purple flowers, has been associated with royalty throughout its long history. The ancient Egyptians used it for perfume, and traces of lavender are said to have been found in the tomb of King Tutankhamun. It was possibly brought to Britain by the Romans, and was certainly growing here by the 13th century.

OPPOSITE
Lavender has long been a royal favourite. By Judith Golder, 2010.

At the Tudor court, lavender's soothing scent saw it gathered into silk bags to lay in or between the sovereign's clothes while they were stored, and placed in among the bedlinen to keep that smelling similarly fresh – the historic precedents for the lavender bags and drawer liners of more modern times. Henry VIII's son, Edward VI, had a 'lavender man' authorised to obtain sufficient soap from the royal spicery for the King's washing, the title of his position reflecting the plant's ancient use in the cleaning of both garments and bodies. It is said to derive its name from the Latin *lavare*, meaning 'to wash'.

Edward's half-sister Elizabeth I is reputed to have used lavender for a different purpose: to help with her recurrent headaches. She was reportedly particularly partial to lavender conserve or jam – a foodstuff prepared, according to the supposedly regal recipe of Queen Henrietta Maria shared in 1655's *The Queens Closet Opened,* with lavender 'flowers being new, so many as you please' beaten 'with three times their weight of white Sugar'. Herbalists of the 16th and 17th centuries certainly did recommend lavender for 'all the griefes and paines of the head' and to 'comfort the braine' (if the flowers were quilted in a cap worn everyday), though firm evidence that Elizabeth I actually medicated with lavender in a conserve or any other form is harder to find.

By the early 1800s, lavender water was being used as perfume by George IV (who spent vast sums on smelling pleasant), while his niece Queen Victoria was purportedly a 'great believer in lavender as a disinfectant', and, as a result, the royal residences were 'strongly impregnated with the refreshing odour' of what the late-Victorian reporter of the fact called 'this old-fashioned flower'. Upon Surrey-based lavender distiller (and entrepreneurial businesswoman) Miss Sarah Sprules, her Majesty bestowed the lofty title of 'Purveyor of Lavender Essence to the Queen' in 1886 – an emphatic signalling of her own support for a plant with plenty of royal pedigree.

ABOVE
Lavender growing in the kitchen garden at Hampton Court Palace.

RIGHT
Lavender growing in the Walled Garden at Hillsborough Castle and Gardens in Northern Ireland.

S. Slocock '14

LONICERA

HONEYSUCKLE

Emblematic of constancy, honeysuckle was given by lovers to signal their undying passion – for Henry VIII and Anne Boleyn, unaware of how quickly their union would unravel, it must have seemed the perfect choice for their private motif.

THE HONEYSUCKLE'S NAME DERIVES from the sweet nectar of its flowers, which tempted country children to suck on them. But on account of its habit of twining itself around the branches of other shrubs and trees, it was commonly known as woodbine (or woodbyne) in the 1530s, when Henry wooed and wed the woman for whom he cast off both his first queen, Katherine of Aragon, and his Catholic faith.

A plant that the Victorians preferred to leave outdoors, for fear that its sweet and heady scent – which only gets stronger at night – would give their daughters passionate dreams, Henry brought it into the palace in its symbolic form. His and Anne's motif, which combined honeysuckle with acorns (a symbol of fertility) and the initials 'H' and 'A' woven together, was soon embedded into the architecture, especially at Hampton Court, and splashed over all manner of furniture and furnishings, from carpets and cushions to bed hangings.

As the honeysuckle spread its tendrils across the royal estate, all traces of the rather less romantic pomegranate – Katherine's badge and the symbol of the city of Granada in her native Spain – were pushed aside. With showy orange flowers that turn into delicious fruit, the pomegranate also promised fertility, but had painfully failed to deliver for the ousted Queen the son and heir that her husband so desperately desired; of six children born to the couple, only their daughter Mary survived. Perhaps for all those concerned

OPPOSITE
The pretty honeysuckle was also known as woodbine in Tudor England. By Shirley Slocock, 2014.

with her exile from court, the reminder of what might have been was best swept away.

By contrast, the honeysuckle, redolent of love-struck summer evenings, spoke powerfully of Henry's hopes for his new start. But the flower's nectar-rich blooms distract from something more dangerous; in the autumn, they give way to toxic berries, just as Henry's infatuation with Anne soon gave way to disappointment and distrust.

The marriage produced just a single daughter, Elizabeth, and after a couple of miscarriages, and amid accusations of adultery, Henry's second queen ended up on the executioner's block in 1536. Thereafter, Anne's honeysuckle suffered the same treatment as Katherine's pomegranate; the disillusioned Henry set out to remove the more prominent examples. That said, a pomegranate remains carved onto a doorway in the Great Hall at Hampton Court, and Katherine and Henry's daughter would also later adopt the pomegranate as her own emblem when she came to the throne as Mary I in 1553.

Though not for Anne, generally honeysuckle has been considered lucky in centuries past. When planted near the entrance to a house, or draped around garden gates, it was thought to stop evil spirits from entering and to encourage good fortune. In the 20th century, the late Queen Mother liked to do just that, not so much for luck but for fragrance. It is well known that the honeysuckle's 'ivory bugles blow scent instead of sound', or that's how Samuel Pepys in a poetic mood once put it. Queen Elizabeth II had two plants placed either side of the front door at Sandringham so that the honeysuckle's joyous scent would surround her the very moment she stepped outside.

ABOVE
Henry VIII's first wife, Katherine of Aragon, by Lucas Horenbout, c. 1525.

ABOVE
A 16th-century woodcut showing the coronation of Henry and Katherine in 1509 includes the pomegranate alongside the Tudor rose, taken from *A Joyful Meditation of the Coronation of King Henry the Eighth* by Stephen Hawes.

ABOVE
The moment Henry VIII met his future wife, Anne Boleyn, imagined in a painting of 1835 by Daniel Maclise.

Matricaria Chamomilla

Chamomile

Chamomile has a reputation for healing. Known as the 'plant physician' for its ability to revive ailing crops when grown alongside them, and long cherished by humans for its soothing capabilities, royals are among those intrigued by its medicinal powers.

Its sunny, summer blossoming flowers were, for instance, a regular ingredient in Henry VIII's medical remedies, including one he devised himself during a stay at Hampton Court Palace: a 'Pusset Oyntment' for the healing of skin sores. These were perhaps the persistent and painful leg ulcers that long troubled the King, and for which chamomile, with its calming and anti-inflammatory properties, would certainly have offered some relief. But whether it had any effect on Henry's skin in combination with the other ingredients of his self-concocted 'oyntment' – which included a lead compound and 'unicorn horn' (probably actually horn from a narwhal) – unfortunately, we don't know.

The handwritten book of remedies from the early 1540s, in which it appears, is not the only historical document from the Royal Household in which a tiny glimpse of the daisy-like chamomile flower can be found. As far back as 1313, the wardrobe accounts of the later-dethroned King Edward II show the purchase of chamomile plants, presumed to be for the purpose of freshening his clothes and rooms.

In the 17th century, the writer of *The Queens Closet Opened*, the personal secretary to Charles I's consort, Henrietta

OPPOSITE
'Henry VIII and the Barber Surgeons' (detail), 1540, by Hans Holbein the Younger.

Maria, purported to spill the domestic secrets of the by-then-exiled Queen through a series of recipes for both cures and cookery, and one such recipe features chamomile in a remedy 'for Heat or scurfe in the Face'. Mixed up with cream, the chamomile was boiled to make a balm, which perhaps the Queen used, as instructed, to 'anoint the face'. The plant certainly played a small role in the beauty regime of another royal. Queen Victoria's dressers were directed to have a bowl of chamomile tea waiting in the dressing room when she changed for dinner in the evenings for their mistress to bathe her presumably tired eyes.

Victoria was the first sovereign to host one of the garden parties that are now staples of the British royal calendar, and chamomile features in their story, too. A non-flowering variety of the plant forms a fragrant area of the main lawn at Buckingham Palace, creating a wonderfully scented stage set for the annual parties, because when trodden underfoot or sodden after a rain shower, chamomile releases the sweet, fruity fragrance that is responsible for its name. It derives from the Greek for 'earth apple' or, more literally, 'apple of the ground'.

Thought to have been planted in the palace garden at some point in the 19th century, the patch puts to the test the maxim of Shakespeare's Falstaff about chamomile – that 'the more it is trodden on, the faster it grows'. Whether that is true or not, unlike conventional grass, the chamomile lawn certainly retains its fresh, green colour even in the hottest and driest of summers, the latest in a long line of services the multi-talented chamomile has rendered to the royals.

OPPOSITE TOP
A painting by Frederick Sargent depicting a garden party at Buckingham Palace, 1887.

OPPOSITE BOTTOM
The manuscript containing medical remedies devised by Henry VIII and his physicians in the 1540s.

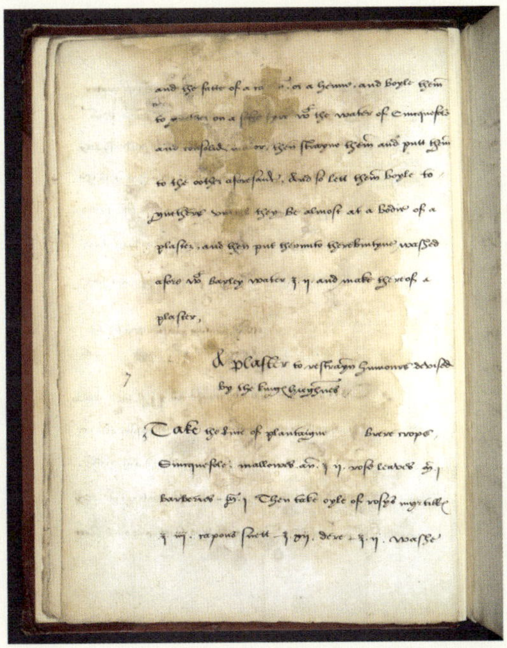

and the [illegible] of a [illegible] or a henne, and boyle them
to [illegible] on a [illegible] fyer wt the water of Cinquefoile
and [illegible] [illegible], then strayne them and putt them
to the other aforesaid, And so lett them boyle to
[illegible] [illegible] they be almost at a bodie of a
plaster, and then put thereunto therebintyne wasshed
afore wt barley water ℥ ij and make thereof a
plaster,

A plaster to restrayn humours devised
by the kings highnes

7 Take the [illegible] of plantaigne [illegible] ropes,
Cinquefoile, mallowes an. ℥ ij. rose leaves [illegible]
barberies [illegible] Then take oyle of roses myrtille
℥ iij. rapons [illegible] ℥ vj. [illegible] ℥ ij. wasshe

D. Blair F.L.S. ad nat. del. et lith.

MORUS NIGRA, *Linn.*

M & N. Hanhart imp.

Morus

Mulberry

Famous from the old nursery rhyme, the mulberry tree is forever associated with the failed efforts of an enterprising 17th-century royal.

PROBABLY INTRODUCED TO OUR SHORES BY THE ROMANS, by the time of the Tudors, those who had mulberries growing in the garden were envied for the juicy, deep-purple berries they could harvest for the dinner table. But it was the knowledge that silkworms feed on the glossy leaves of the mulberry tree that so excited King James VI of Scotland & I of England in the early 17th century.

To James, the son of Mary, Queen of Scots, and the first monarch to rule both countries, the idea of cultivating mulberries on an industrial scale, and thereby covering himself in glory by reducing the country's reliance on expensive, imported yarn and growing a silk industry to rival that of the French, had enormous appeal.

To that end, around 1608 he imported thousands of saplings from the Continent, and planted them in a four-acre royal garden on the site of what later became Buckingham Palace. No expense was spared, and dedicated Mulberry Men were even employed to tend them. Trees were also planted at Theobalds Palace in Hertfordshire, and at the royal residence of Oatlands in Surrey, where his wife Anne of Denmark oversaw the creation of a grand two-storey house purely for the keeping and warming of silkworms, under the supervision of a dedicated keeper.

OPPOSITE
Illustration of the *Morus nigra* black mulberry by David Blair, 1880. Taken from *Medicinal Plants* by Henry Trimen and Robert Bentley.

Not content with developing this grand enterprise on his own lands, the King wrote to all his Lord Lieutenants, too, urging them to encourage every landowner with the means to purchase mulberries. Many of them did, leading to a scattering of trees, everywhere from Cambridge colleges to great country estates. Shakespeare is thought to have been among those who heeded the call, planting one in his garden in Stratford-upon-Avon.

Regrettably, despite the King's enthusiasm, the great garden scheme proved to be a washout. Some say it was because most of the plants ordered by his gardeners were black mulberries, rather than the white variety preferred by silkworms. But the damp and chilly climate of James' kingdom was probably more of a problem. London, in the grip of what's been called the Little Ice Age, was so cold in the winter of 1608 that the Thames froze over. The weather in subsequent years did not improve and his mulberry trees, sensitive to frost, did not thrive. The lyrics of the famous nursery rhyme, 'here we go round the mulberry bush, on a cold and frosty morning' might, in fact, be a nod to the lessons learned from King James' great royal experiment, which never produced any great quantity of silk, and was largely abandoned within little more than a decade. By the 1650s, the London mulberry garden for which he had such high hopes was known only as a pleasure garden, later frequented by the great diarist Samuel Pepys.

It doesn't take long for a mulberry tree to develop a gnarled appearance suggestive of great age, leading to speculation that some of the original royal mulberries survived. They have not, but the memory of them lives on, not least because Buckingham Palace is today home to the National Collection of Mulberries – forty different varieties, including cultivars of the *Morus alba* white mulberry that would have tempted King James' silkworms. The fruits of the trees are harvested by hand in June and July every year, and then used in the royal kitchens to create crumbles and soufflés. Meanwhile, in more ordinary gardens, many of those who tend a mulberry will be growing the 'King James' variety, derived from the last remaining tree planted in his reign and by far the most popular variety today.

OPPOSITE
Portrait believed to be of James VI and I's wife Anne of Denmark, wearing a dress embroidered with silkworms. Unknown artist, c. 1600.

OPPOSITE
King James VI of Scotland and I of England, by Daniel Mytens, 1621.

ABOVE
A mulberry tree in the gardens of Buckingham Palace.

ABOVE
King Richard II surrenders his crown to Henry of Lancaster, the future King Henry IV, by Jean Froissart, c. 1470–72.

Myosotis

Forget-me-not

Opportunistic usurper of the English throne, it is thought that Henry IV chose the forget-me-not for a personal emblem.

Best known for small, pretty blooms of vivid blue that come back year after year, the forget-me-not perhaps acquired its association with fidelity and constancy – and thus its cult status with lovers – thanks to its resilience. It's a famously hardy plant that thrives even, as 16th-century botanist John Gerard put it, on the 'most drie gravely and barren ditch bankes'.

Its tenacity made it an appropriate choice for the future Henry IV. The son of the Lancastrian John of Gaunt, Henry was, in fact, an inconvenient two places down the line of succession to the crown. His eventual accession was largely prompted by the vindictive treatment he suffered at the hands of the King, his cousin, Richard II. Amid accusations of treason, Richard sent Henry into exile in France in 1398 and confiscated his vast estates.

The flower the exiled Henry is traditionally thought to have taken as a personal emblem he knew as '*souveyne vous de moi*' – 'remember me' – but it is likely to be the bloom we know today as the forget-me-not, which only actually acquired the more poetic moniker a couple or more centuries later. Henry's accounts books show that the flowers were incorporated into his clothes and livery chains, from gowns, mantles and collars to a belt formed from a trail of them, 'hanging copiously with gilded silver leaves and fronds'. When he was exiled to the Continent,

Henry's extremely prominent emblem said everything it needed to. The English were hardly able to forget him, for his return came swiftly; in 1399 he invaded England, successfully forced the surrender and abdication of the unpopular King Richard, and usurped the throne, all while casually disregarding the claims of the acknowledged heir. The forget-me-not, somewhat inappropriately modest and easily overshadowed for such a king, remained connected with him until his death in 1413.

But Henry himself would eventually be usurped in the forget-me-not story, when nearly 600 years later, the flower was revealed to be the favourite of another royal, one of modern history's most memorable, Princess Diana.

An unshowy choice, not fashionable or rare, nor requiring the resources of a royal to cultivate, it was unknown to her sons until it was revealed by the Spencer family to the gardeners at Kensington Palace, her former home, in 2016. The fact that Prince Harry had named the charity he co-founded with Prince Seeiso of Lesotho 'Sentebale' – which means 'forget me not' in the country's official language – was a pure coincidence, based on the pair's shared desire to honour their much-missed mothers and their own work with those affected by AIDS and poverty.

In more recent times, both of Diana's sons have turned to the dainty flower to consciously honour her memory. On the morning of his wedding to Meghan Markle in 2018, Prince Harry handpicked stems of a white variety from the couple's garden to include in her bridal bouquet, and for the first Buckingham Palace garden party after the coronation of his father in 2023, Prince William chose tiny blue forget-me-nots for his buttonhole. The flower also featured prominently in a 2021 re-design of Kensington Palace's peaceful sunken garden, to commemorate what would have been Princess Diana's 60th birthday.

ABOVE
The sunken garden at Kensington Palace is filled with some of the favourite flowers of the late Princess Diana.

ABOVE
Portrait of King Henry IV of England (1367-1413) by an unknown artist, c. 1600.

Myrtus Communis

Myrtle

From Queen Victoria's eldest daughter to the current Princess of Wales, since 1858 many royal brides have chosen to walk down the aisle carrying a sprig of myrtle in their bouquet.

THIS DELICATE FLOWER, cultivated in Britain since the 1500s, has been connected with love since Roman times and adorned bridalwear for centuries. The time-honoured royal tradition, however, has its origins in a small posy of the showy, summer-flowering white blooms presented to Queen Victoria by Prince Albert's grandmother, at the end of a trip to his native Germany in September 1845.

The young Queen, a true romantic and no doubt well aware that in the fashionable 'language of flowers' myrtle was the emblem of love, brought it back to plant in the grounds of Osborne House, their newly acquired holiday estate on the Isle of Wight. Then, almost thirteen years later, when her eldest daughter, also Victoria, married Crown Prince Frederick of Prussia, the Queen had a sprig cut from Osborne's flourishing myrtle shrubs for her bridal bouquet, and from that sprig, another plant was grown.

As *The Times* newspaper reported in 1863, after the wedding of Victoria's son and heir, Albert Edward, to Princess Alexandra of Denmark – whose own bridal myrtle, in her bouquet and on her dress, came courtesy of the shrub grown from her sister-in-law Princess Vicky's wedding flowers – it was the Queen's plan to raise myrtles from each of the family's bridal bouquets, 'in remembrance of these auspicious events'. The sentimental scheme not only made myrtle

OPPOSITE
Illustration of myrtle by William Clark, 1833.

synonymous with royal wedding celebrations, but resulted in a proliferation of the plants at Osborne, where the Queen delighted in their 'quite delicious' scent on summer evenings. Descendants of the original plants thrive there today, still found on the Italianate terraces where they grew in her lifetime.

Victoria chose and sent cuttings from them for family nuptials far and wide during her reign, from Berlin to St Petersburg. And it is the Osborne myrtle bushes that have provided sprigs for almost all royal bridal bouquets in recent memory, including those of Queen Elizabeth II, Princess Diana, Catherine, Princess of Wales and Meghan, Duchess of Sussex. With myrtle blooming only in late summer, the sprigs typically bear just fragrant, dark-green foliage, usually combined with all-white flowers; lily of the valley has been a perennially popular choice.

The custom of sending the family's bridal bouquets to Westminster Abbey, to be laid on the tomb of the Unknown Warrior, is a more recent one. It was started by the late Queen Mother, who chose myrtle for the wreath in her hair rather than her bouquet when she married the future King George VI in 1923. Perhaps inspired by her sister-in-law Princess Mary, who had stopped her carriage by the Cenotaph on Whitehall to lay flowers after her wedding the previous year, she stepped aside to place her bridal posy on the tombstone as she waited to walk down the Abbey's aisle. Approving onlookers speculated that it was a personal and spontaneous gesture, done in memory of her brother Fergus, killed at the Battle of Loos in 1915, but it started a new tradition. Nearly every royal bride in the subsequent generations has carried out the same act of remembrance, albeit usually sending their bouquets back to the Abbey after the wedding.

A similarly poignant note was struck when myrtle was included in the wreath that adorned the late Queen's coffin at her state funeral in September 2022. Chosen to represent her long, happy marriage to Prince Philip, in a respectful echo of the Victorian tradition, it was cut from a myrtle plant grown from the sprig her late Majesty carried in her own wedding bouquet in 1947.

ABOVE
Albert Edward, Prince of Wales, and Princess Alexandra of Denmark on their wedding day, 10 March 1863. By Amedee Forestier, 1901.

LEFT
Myrtle bushes in the grounds of Osborne House have provided sprigs for the bouquets of royal brides past and present.

BRANDARD. CHAPEL ROYAL, St JAMES'S M & N. HANHART, IMP.

OPPOSITE
The marriage of Victoria, the Princess Royal, and Prince Frederick of Prussia on 25 January 1858. By Michael Hanhart, 1858.

ABOVE
Myrtle growing on the Italianate terraces at Osborne House.

PAPAVER

Poppy

Every November for the past century, the Royal Family, like many Britons, have worn red poppies to honour the service and sacrifice of those who have lost their lives in war.

THE IDEA OF TURNING THE POPPY, a vibrant staple of our summer meadows, into a symbol of wartime remembrance, associated with the autumn months, actually originated in America, and was inspired by the words of a poem, *In Flanders Fields*, written in 1915 by a Canadian officer who served in the First World War on the Western Front. Much like those who lived through the Napoleonic Wars and saw carpets of blood-red poppies springing up where the Battle of Waterloo had been fought and thousands of soldiers had fallen, Colonel John McCrae had noticed that among the mud and misery,

'In Flanders Fields the poppies blow
Between the crosses, row on row.'

His sorrowful verses, that warned 'If ye break faith with us who die, we shall not sleep', stirred an American academic to begin a campaign to make the poppy the nation's symbol of remembrance. It was a call that chimed with the leader of a French charity, Anna Guérin, who had crossed the Atlantic with artificial poppies to sell to raise funds for war widows and orphans. Spurred on by success with the venture Stateside, Guérin soon brought them to Britain, where the fledgling Royal British Legion ordered nine million of her French-made fabric blooms as a way of fundraising for their own work.

It was Queen Mary, consort of King George V, who was our first royal to embrace the emblem, buying two of Britain's very

OPPOSITE
King Charles lays a wreath of poppies at the Cenotaph on Whitehall on Remembrance Sunday.

first remembrance poppies from sellers she asked to call at Buckingham Palace on their very first day on sale, 11 November 1921. That year, by command of the King, the wreath he laid at the Cenotaph featured what the papers were calling 'Flanders Poppies', as did that of the Prince of Wales.

It is a tradition that has continued largely unchanged for over a century, with the royals proudly wearing their poppies in the lead-up to Remembrance Day in November. To this day, the royals also remain involved with the Royal British Legion, an organisation that began employing veterans to manufacture their own poppies in Britain from 1922. Queen Camilla is patron of their Poppy Factory in Richmond, where the paper flowers for the annual campaign are still made more than 100 years on.

The resilient field poppy may have honourable associations with the British royals, but its enigmatic cousin, the paler opium poppy, has also been – less edifyingly – entwined in the history of the British crown. The most accessible drug of the Georgian era, cheaper than either beer or gin, it was astonishingly easy to buy in the over-the-counter liquid preparation, laudanum, a potent mix of opium and spirits. The future King George IV began taking laudanum around the time he took to the throne as Regent in 1811, having reportedly been first prescribed it as a painkiller after twisting his ankle demonstrating the Highland Fling – presumably with a bit too much enthusiasm for a man of his size and sedentary habits. By the late 1820s, many might describe him as an addict, routinely taking hundreds of drops a day before public appearances, alongside vast quantities of brandy.

His intake was far in excess of a routine dose and near-enough entire days could pass with the British sovereign in a drug-induced stupor. Either that, or he was asleep for hours, and so agitated and irritable when the effects of his opium wore off that his ministers were advised to stay away. Some blamed the royal doctors for letting it go so far; many more the notoriously self-indulgent King himself.

ABOVE
Queen Mary, the wife of King George V.

ABOVE AND OPPOSITE
The Duke and Duchess of Cambridge, Prince Harry, the late Queen and Prince Philip walk among the thousands of ceramic poppies installed at the Tower of London in 2014 to mark the centenary of the outbreak of the First World War.

Primula veris

Cowslip

As Charles II lay on his deathbed in 1685, among the multitude of remedies his twelve attending physicians resorted to was a powder of cowslip flowers – an attempt to 'strengthen' his brain in the wake of a series of alarming seizures.

Known as 'palsywort' to some, the cheery, zingy-yellow cowslip had been recommended as a cure for palsy and paralysis since the medieval period, the thinking seemingly being that the flower's trembling heads would make it beneficial for shaking limbs. As they scrambled desperately to treat him, the King's physicians appear to have been following the confident endorsements of herbalists like Nicholas Culpeper, who claimed the flower not just as a cure for convulsions but for 'all infirmities of the head'.

Unfortunately, despite the flower's medicinal pedigree, the cowslip failed to save the beleaguered Charles, as did all fifty or more of the other treatments, botanical-based, bizarre and otherwise, that were pushed upon him. He died after four days of illness, probably of kidney failure.

The delicate cowslip, considered fit to treat a king, actually takes its name from the decidedly indelicate 'cowslop' (cow-pat), for it flourished in cattle fields and other grasslands. Native to British shores, it was once very common as a wild flower, growing abundantly in our hay meadows, on hillsides and in hedgerows, but it fell into catastrophic decline as its natural habitats disappeared. It is this part of its story that connects it with the next Charles to reign, our current King.

OPPOSITE
The flourishing wildflower meadow at Highgrove House in Gloucestershire, which was purchased by King Charles in 1980.

A passionate advocate for the environment from his early adulthood, Charles became alarmed by what he described as 'the appalling short-sighted damage done to the soil, the landscape and our own souls' by our modern way of life. So much so, that when he purchased the neo-classical Highgrove House in Gloucestershire and its accompanying 300-acre estate in 1980, he was determined not only to make it entirely organic, but to create from scratch a wildflower meadow to encourage our native flora and fauna.

Biodiversity expert Miriam Rothschild was tasked with helping the then Prince of Wales to develop a specialised thirty-two-species seed mix for hand-sowing. They dubbed it 'the Gloucestershire Farmer's Nightmare'. Now, just over forty years on, the cowslip's tall and gently nodding yellow heads are some of the most prominent and joyful of a whole host of native blooms that burst into life there every spring.

Both the King's passion for meadows – which he has described as 'at once intoxicating and restorative' when seen in all their summer glory – and the spectacular display at Highgrove, have encouraged many to follow his lead. Most especially through his 2012 'Coronation Meadows' project, which aimed to celebrate the 60th anniversary of his mother's coronation by creating at least one new wildflower meadow in every county of Britain, using seeds from a surviving one. More recently, 2022 saw the Tower of London transform its famous moat from flat lawn to flower-filled landscape in honour of Elizabeth II's platinum jubilee; and for Charles' own coronation the following year, primary schools across the country were sent packets of wildflower seeds, to allow them to do the same for a small patch of their local ground.

Early indications are that awareness of the need to act is making a difference. The cowslip, once as common as the buttercup, is at last slowly returning to our countryside, and the King can rightly claim some of the credit.

ABOVE
Wild flowers adorned the invitation for the coronation of King Charles and Queen Camilla in 2023.

THE ROYAL OAK.

The Penderell Family have no idea where Charles is!!!

QUERCUS

OAK

—

The most quintessentially British of all trees, there are more ancient oaks in Britain than in all the countries of Europe combined. And the mighty oak has a particularly special place in the annals of our royal history.

WE TALK, OF COURSE, OF THE BOSCOBEL OAK; the tree where the future King Charles II hid from Cromwell's Parliamentarian soldiers after his attempt to invade England and reclaim his father's throne had ended in defeat at the Battle of Worcester.

The deposed royal arrived in Shropshire mere hours after the battle in September 1651 and, at first, an attempt was made to help him escape into Wales on foot. But when it became clear that all routes were heavily guarded, he was taken instead to the remote Boscobel House, a one-time hiding place for Catholic priests, shrouded in dense woodlands. As the Roundheads closed in on the area, Charles acquiesced to the suggestion that he and a fellow fugitive clamber up into the boughs of a 'great oak' that was 'grown out very bushy and thick not to be seen through', and there wait out the inevitable search. From dawn till dusk, they sat in its branches, never spotted by Cromwell's troops. After his pursuers had departed, with the protection of royalist subjects, Charles was able to travel onwards to the coast, making for the safety of the Continent, where he spent almost a decade in exile.

In his absence, the oak tree and its acorns became symbols of loyalty to the first 'king over the water', and on his restoration to the throne in 1660, Charles himself ensured that the oak became part of the rich tapestry of royal history, telling and

OPPOSITE
The royalist Penderel family helped Charles II to hide from the Parliamentarians in the branches of a great oak tree, by John Leech, 1880.

re-telling the story of the events at Boscobel. The date of his triumphant return to London, the 29th May, became 'Oak Apple Day' – a day of thanksgiving for the Stuart dynasty's deliverance. A public holiday in Britain until 1859, the pensioners of the Royal Hospital Chelsea, founded by Charles II, still mark the anniversary every year, pinning oak leaves to their iconic scarlet tunics, and adorning his statue with branches of oak.

Famously, English oaks have an immensely long life-span and the UK is home to a vast number of ancient oak trees, many hundreds of years old; there is an oak still growing in Windsor Great Park that was rooted in its soil decades before William the Conqueror started building the Castle in around 1070. Sadly, the Boscobel Oak is not of their number. After the Restoration, it became a popular place of pilgrimage, and so intent were royalist souvenir-hunters on taking a piece of living history home with them, that by the early 1700s so much had been cut away that it was all but dead. The tree that stands there today (in the care of English Heritage) is an offspring of the original. Other direct descendants thrive in royal soil, in the Meadow at Highgrove House. They were presented to our current King Charles by the Forestry Commission and the Tree Council on the occasion of his marriage to Lady Diana Spencer in 1981.

The royal roots of the majestic-looking oak neither begin nor end with Charles II, however. A venerable tree in Nottinghamshire was said to be the site of a meeting of Parliament convened by Edward I in 1290, and Henry VI reputedly slept under a great oak in the grounds of Irton Hall in Cumbria one night during the Wars of the Roses, having been refused sanctuary at the house, which was owned by a Yorkist sympathiser.

Later, legend has it that the pollarded oaks in Leicestershire's Bradgate Park, close to the ruins of the ancestral home of the 'Nine Day Queen' Lady Jane Grey, were 'beheaded' by locals as a mark of respect after she lost her own head on the executioner's block at the Tower of London in 1554. And according to tradition, Queen Elizabeth I was sitting under an oak tree when the news of her half-sister Mary's death and her own accession to the throne were brought to her at Hatfield House in 1558. Another old oak in the park at Greenwich Palace was reportedly one of her favourite summer picnic spots.

Folklore has long linked one more notable sovereign with an oak, too. As word spread of George III's descent into so-called 'madness' in 1788, a tale circulated of him stopping his carriage in Windsor Great Park and shaking hands with the branches of an oak tree in the mistaken belief that it was the King of Prussia. It is a report repeated to this day, despite almost certainly being the baseless fabrication of a news hack.

Today's royals are more likely to be found planting commemorative oak trees, including a replacement for Elizabeth I's famous Hatfield oak tree, which had died by the mid-20th century.

ABOVE
King Charles shown hiding from the Roundheads in the branches of 'a great oak'.

ABOVE
Detail from a portrait of Charles II, painted soon after his successful escape from England by Philippe de Champaigne, 1653.

THE ROYAL VISIT TO LEICESTER: THE PRINCESS OF WALES PLANTING AN OAK IN THE ABBEY PARK.

ABOVE
Alexandra, Princess of Wales, plants a young oak tree to mark the opening of Leicester's Abbey Park in 1882, from *The Illustrated London News*.

ABOVE
King George VI and Queen Elizabeth at the Chelsea Flower Show in 1938.

Rhododendron

Rhododendron

A keen gardener – like his grandson, Charles III – King George VI became an authority on his favourite plant of all, the rhododendron.

It may not be a fashionable shrub today, dismissed by some as excessively gaudy and despised by others on ecological grounds, but the rhododendron was all the rage in the interwar years when George VI went from spare to heir, thanks to his brother Edward VIII's abdication in 1936. The favourite of the smart set and a must-have for country seats, the Chelsea Flower Show of the era was always stuffed full of colourful and exotic varieties.

This bright and bountiful plant had been brought to Britain in the 18th century, when it first found royal favour, being among the exotics Queen Charlotte had sent over from the botanic garden at Kew to fill her new flowerbeds at Frogmore House in the 1790s. But it wasn't until the late 1800s that a craze for rhododendrons – meaning 'rose trees' in Greek – swept the country, as ever-more intrepid plant hunters began to carry back home rare varieties, first from the Himalayas, then from China, which were later bred into fashionable hybrids.

By the 1930s, when George VI began planting them in his garden at Royal Lodge in Windsor Great Park – the country house that was intended to be his and the late Queen Mother's 'real home' – there was already one rhododendrophile in the Royal Family. The more glamorous Edward, then Prince of Wales, had already added a woodland-style rhododendron garden at his own country pad, Fort Belvedere, with a host of handsome Himalayan hybrids. He had also become patron of the Rhododendron Association.

But it was the quieter, more dutiful 'Bertie' (as George VI was known to his family) who acquired an exceptional knowledge of the shrub and its species. 'Nobody could stump him!' declared a contemporary expert. At Royal Lodge he created a rhododendron walk where visitors could admire the great clouds of their colourful blooms, along with a dedicated species garden. Later, during his reign, they were followed by a spectacular display in the Great Park's Valley Gardens, where the rare varieties collected by aficionado J. B. Stevenson and purchased by the royals from his widow, found a new home.

Not everyone was so pleased to see them sprouting everywhere. One of the couple's long-time gardeners was eventually moved to request a palace-issue boiler suit for the 'long dirty sticky job' of picking the rhododendron blooms. 'I have to get right inside some of them … and I get in a very dirty mess – much to the annoyance of Mrs P. when it comes to washing day,' Ernest Pearce wrote in support of his claim.

But the King, like his grandson, was prepared to get his own hands dirty; willing to get stuck in with planting, and to wield a saw for pruning. Gardening no doubt provided a much-needed outlet for the stresses and strains of the role of sovereign, the part he had never expected to have to play. His son-in-law Prince Philip certainly recalled one occasion when, arriving at Royal Lodge, and wandering out to the garden to find the King, he was greeted by a tirade of obscenities emanating from a rhododendron bush. He discovered his father-in-law hacking away at it, swearing – all while wearing his Guardsman's bearskin, which Andrew Wallis, curator of the Guards Museum, speculates was an attempt to acclimatise to wearing the hat before the Trooping of the Colour.

Another story has the King, on a visit during the Second World War to Hampshire's Exbury House, which had been requisitioned by the Admiralty, wandering off down its justifiably famous rhododendron walks, somewhat to the surprise of the naval officers conducting him on his inspection. Exbury's owner Lionel de Rothschild reportedly described himself as 'a banker by hobby and a gardener by profession' – a sentiment that perhaps the rhododendron's greatest royal enthusiast could empathise with.

ABOVE
Bright and bountiful rhododendron bushes took root in the royal gardens in the early 20th century – this one is in the gardens of Hillsborough Castle.

ABOVE
The famous 'Pelican Portrait' of Elizabeth I is awash with roses. By Nicholas Hilliard, 1572.

Rosa

Rose

The rose has been known as the 'queen of flowers' since at least the 2nd century CE, so it seems only fitting that of all blooms it is the one most entwined with the crown.

THIS ELEGANT AND FAMOUSLY RICHLY SCENTED FLOWER is one of the oldest continually cultivated plants in the world. Yet while King Edward I of England is said to have used a golden rose as one of his emblems as early as the 13th century, its regal connection really only begins with the Wars of the Roses in the mid-1400s.

Both the rival houses of York and Lancaster, who spent three decades fighting for the English Crown, had roses among their family emblems, the story goes – white and red ones respectively, so that 'between the red rose and white' were sent, as Shakespeare wrote, 'a thousand souls to death and deadly night.' The long-running war ended in victory for the Lancastrians at the Battle of Bosworth in 1485, with Henry Tudor taking the throne as King Henry VII. As the new ruler of a divided nation, Henry's marriage to Elizabeth of York, the daughter of the former Yorkist King, Edward IV, was an important step in securing his crown. Their wedding, in 1486, not only united their two once-warring families and their claims to the throne, but created the Tudor rose, an apparent merger of their families' distinctive red and white emblems, with its five red outer petals surrounding five white inner ones.

It was a masterful piece of dynastic 'branding' – especially as it was more fiction than fact. While the white rose, adopted by the House of York a couple of decades before the conflict began, was ubiquitous, the Lancastrians began to use the red rose only very late on. Still, the Tudor rose allowed the new King to frame a long and complicated war, involving brutality, betrayal and his dubious claim to the throne, as a straightforward tale of two divided families, now united in one dynasty. On his watch, the Tudor rose came to represent peace and stability, and even England itself. However, it is arguable that the association with England was already established; in Roman times, Pliny the Elder thought that the country derived the name of 'Albion' – from the Latin *albus,* meaning 'white' – perhaps from either the distinctive white cliffs of Dover, or its abundant white roses.

At the Tudor court, it would have certainly been hard to avoid the flower, which Henry VII and his successors deployed liberally to help shore up their dynasty and promote their legitimacy. The King, his wife, and his son and heir Henry VIII, were all painted clasping roses. The latter scattered the Tudor rose over all manner of his possessions, and sprinkled them generously across the architecture and décor of his royal palaces. They were carved into the woodwork, painted onto ceilings and adorned stained glass windows, especially at Hampton Court where they can still be seen today.

All three of Henry VIII's legitimate children would also be painted with roses, though none more so than Elizabeth. The 'Pelican Portrait' of around 1575 is absolutely awash with roses – not just the giant Tudor rose hovering above the Queen's shoulder, but the red bloom pinned to her bodice, the jewelled flowers on her skirt, the outlines dotted over her undershirt, and the enormous feather fan shaped like a rose, which just clips the edge of the canvas.

As Queen, Elizabeth also chose a rose for her personal symbol – specifically the wild, five-petalled 'eglantine' (or sweet briar) rose, which had been the symbol of her paternal grandmother and namesake, Elizabeth of York. It was an assertion of her Tudor heritage, not to mention being imbued with some very useful symbolism for an unmarried female monarch: the rose had long been associated with the Virgin Mary and thus emphasised Elizabeth's chastity.

The eglantine rose appeared on coinage, cropped up time and again in literature, and was planted by courtiers

ABOVE
Henry Tudor and his bride Elizabeth of York, holding the red and white roses associated with their once-warring families, by Sarah, Countess of Essex, 1825.

RIGHT
The rose was the centrepiece of a charitable campaign set up in honour of Queen Alexandra, wife of Edward VII.

anxious to express their devotion to the Queen in floral form. Robert Devereux, the Earl of Essex – a young and handsome favourite of Elizabeth in her later life – is believed to be the unnamed man who commissioned a miniature portrait of himself leaning against a tree-trunk entwined with pretty white eglantines; a painting that must once have formed part of a fan or a looking glass, and whose recipient could only have been the Queen.

In the reign of both Elizabeth and her father, however, the roses we know and love for their beauty, served practical as well as dynastic purposes. Both the Queen and her father Henry used rose oil as a scent, and the royal court used bucketfuls of rose water, which was splashed about the palaces to disguise unpleasant smells in the same way as strewing herbs. A mixture of rose water and sugar used in the apartments of Henry VIII's son Edward was said to give off a scent so exhilarating it was as if they were full of the flowers. Moreover, rose water featured in medicinal remedies and flavoured Tudor confectionary, so it would also have been a fixture in the royal kitchens.

As well as the world's favourite flower, the fragrant rose is also, of course, the bloom most associated with love and romance – a marriage some say was made in ancient Egypt, when Cleopatra carpeted the floor of her boudoir with rose petals to woo Mark Antony. And for royals, the rose has certainly had its romantic associations. Henry II would reputedly meet his famously beautiful mistress, 'Fair Rosamund' Clifford, at a rose bower in the grounds of the royal residence of Woodstock in the 1160s and 70s. Legend has it that the Old Rose, *Rosa mundi*, variety of the flower is named for her.

Rather more touching is the story of King Edward VII and his wife Alexandra of Denmark. On the day that the future king proposed to her in the garden of the Belgian palace of Laeken, she gave him two red roses. It was only the couple's second meeting and the match was not one of their own making, but a mutual attraction had been obvious on their introduction a year earlier. And the playboy Prince's heart was clearly engaged too, for he carefully pressed and kept the two blooms, with a note that they were 'from Alix' on the date of their betrothal.

Roses were the favourite of the glamorous young Alexandra. At Sandringham, which had been purchased by

Edward a few months before their marriage in 1863, she later oversaw the creation of a royal 'Rosary' containing some 1,300 varieties, along with a summerhouse, where presumably she could sit and soak up their delicious scent. The rose would also become the centrepiece of the charitable campaign set up in 1912, to mark the 50th anniversary of her first visit to England. 'Alexandra Rose Day' saw thousands of female volunteers, dressed in the Danish national colours, take to the streets to sell silk and linen roses. Made by an organisation supporting disabled women, the purpose was to raise money for London hospitals, a cause that had long been close to the Queen's heart.

A forerunner to the poppy campaign we still see every November, it was initially intended as a one-off occasion, but it became an annual event, raising almost £30 million in today's money by 1920 (and eventually morphing into the Alexandra Rose Charity, which is still supporting Londoners to this day). Despite her increasing deafness and growing reluctance to engage with the world, the enormously popular Alexandra continued to play a starring role in the charity until two years before her death in 1925, driving in an open carriage on a 'radiant progress' through London, stopping to admire stalls beautifully bedecked with roses, and to chat with sellers wending their way through the city streets with trays and collection tins.

Queen Alexandra may have employed the rose as a royal force for good, but it has also been deployed in battles for power – most notably, *Rosa alba,* the white rose, which was adopted by the Jacobites in the 17th and 18th centuries as a symbol of rebellion and resistance against the reigning monarchs.

Supporters of the deposed Catholic King James II and his descendants, the Jacobites refused to accept the 'Glorious Revolution' of 1688, which had put James' Protestant daughter Mary and her husband William of Orange on the British throne. For nearly sixty years, they fought to remove the royals they saw as usurpers and to restore the House of Stuart, initially James II himself, then his son, also James or 'the Old Pretender', and later his grandson, 'Bonnie Prince Charlie' or 'the Young Pretender'.

ABOVE
Prince Charles Edward Stuart, or 'Bonnie Prince Charlie', by Jean-Etienne Liotard, c. 1737.

ABOVE
The Tudor rose visible on the vault of Anne Boleyn's Gateway at Hampton Court Palace.

Though supporters of the royals in exile 'over the water' in France had an array of secret symbols to obscure their treasonous sympathies, the white rose was the one most prominently associated with their cause. One story says that it owes its adoption to the wild bloom that the Young Pretender plucked to adorn his hat when he landed in Scotland ahead of the 1745 'rising', but it was a recognised emblem decades before that. The truth of its selection was probably more pragmatic; the white rose, with its long connection with the House of York, made perfect sense, given that James II had been created Duke of York at his birth, and was known by the title throughout the twenty-five-year reign of his brother Charles II. The fact that the white rose had for centuries also been associated with the Virgin Mary added an extra potency in light of the devout Catholicism shared by James II, his Queen and many of his supporters.

Wearing a white rose in a buttonhole, on a bodice or a hat, became a way of displaying support for the Stuarts, and on no occasion were the blooms more prominent than on the unimaginatively named 'White Rose Day'. Then, Jacobites celebrated the birthday of the Old Pretender: 'of all the days that's in the year, the tenth of June I love most dear … in tartans braw our lads are drest, with roses glancing on their brest' as one of their 'seditious' ballads explained. The white rose, on its own, or in combination with rosebuds to symbolise the succession, was also woven into decorative schemes inside houses, and ornamented everyday possessions, from wine glasses to teapots. More famously, it was transformed into the white cockade that adorned the hats of Jacobites in battle, including in the 1745 rebellion that ended with their final defeat at the Battle of Culloden.

One rose says more than a dozen, the cliche goes, but you would be hard-pressed to find a solitary bloom that could carry more meaning than the abundance of roses in the annals of royal history – from treasonous rebellion to touching romance, power struggles to public relations, they tell of it all.

Rosmarinus officinalis

Published by W. Phillips, Decr. 1st. 1807.

Salvia Rosmarinus

Rosemary

Tradition has it that rosemary, best known today as an aromatic herb for seasoning food, was first brought to these shores by a royal bride, Philippa of Hainault.

Philippa's betrothal to the future king of England was a decidedly unromantic one, the result of a deal between her father and England's Queen Isabella, who wanted financial and military support from Count Willem of Hainault to help her overthrow her husband Edward II. When Isabella succeeded in deposing him and placing their fourteen-year-old son on the throne as Edward III in 1327, she upheld her end of the bargain and Philippa was brought to York to become his Queen.

It was some ten years or so later, the story goes, that while staying at Antwerp, Philippa was sent cuttings of fragrant rosemary by her mother, along with a copy of a treatise proclaiming the plant's many (mainly medicinal) virtues. Both of these she is said to have brought back to England with her.

It was unlikely to be the very first time rosemary had ever been known or grown here; the Romans quite likely carried it with them from the shores of the Mediterranean, which was its native habitat and is reflected in the Latin *Rosmarinus*, which means 'sea dew'. It was known to the Anglo-Saxons, too, for it makes appearances in 'Bald's Leechbook' of the 10th century, which offered everything from charms to medical cures, most of the latter being based around herbs. But the plant, recognisable by its needle-like leaves, had seemingly all but disappeared by the 14th century, and Queen Philippa has long been given the credit for its re-introduction here, perhaps because her cultivation helped to establish it as

OPPOSITE
Hand-coloured engraving of flowered rosemary by James Sowerby, 1832.

a staple of English gardens in the centuries to come.

Like her husband's grandmother Eleanor of Castile, Philippa had a lively interest in gardening. Her rosemary was probably first grown in the Privy Gardens at the Palace of Westminster, chiefly for the medicinal properties extolled in her mother's treatise, which included the power to strengthen bones and prevent nightmares – provided that the person who tried it was free of deadly sin that is, for it was said to be a holy tree. Later English translations of the treatise, possibly drawing on Philippa's experiences of growing rosemary in our cooler climes, added a further advantage. Its leaves were 'evermore green and never falleth', a fact which probably also accounts for its surge in popularity at a time when the English had but a handful of evergreen plants for their gardens.

Rosemary was grown widely by the time Elizabeth I inherited the crown. As she rode in her coronation procession in 1559, a poor woman pressed a humble sprig of it on her somewhere near Fleet Bridge, presumably wishing her to benefit from its renowned ability to ward off evil spirits; the new Queen carried it right beside her into Westminster.

By the end of her reign, rosemary was fairly prolific at Hampton Court Palace, where a visitor in 1598 saw it 'planted and nailed to the walls as to cover them entirely', which, he remarked, was 'a method exceedingly common in England' – no doubt because regularly inhaling the fresh, pungent aroma of rosemary leaves was believed to 'keep thee youngly' and stimulate the mind.

Also strongly associated with remembrance in Tudor times, sprigs of rosemary were a common component of both weddings and funerals. Anne of Cleves approached the altar wearing a glittering coronet of gold and precious stones 'set full of branches of rosemary' for her marriage to Henry VIII in 1540, though by all accounts it was not a day either wanted to remember. Shortly before the ceremony, the King was heard to mutter, 'If it were not to satisfy the world and my realm, I would not do that I must do this day for none earthly thing.' Despite rosemary being purported to have aphrodisiac-like effects – 16th-century readers were urged to carry it to make themselves 'merry, glad [and] well beloved of all men' or to put it in their baths to be a little more 'lusty, lively, joyful, strong and young' – the union between Henry and his fourth wife was annulled just six months later, without the marriage ever having been consummated.

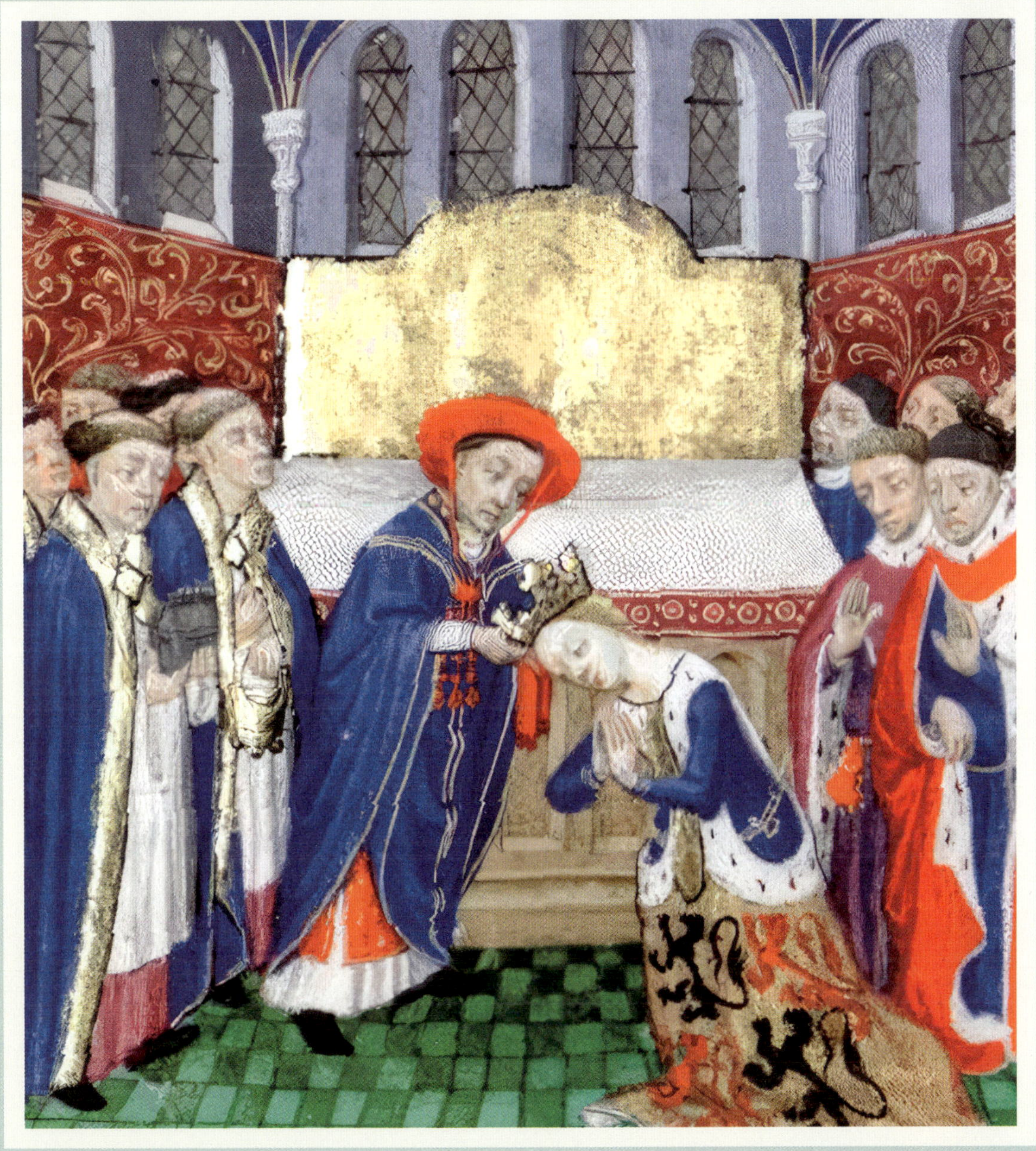

ABOVE
A 15th-century illustration of the coronation of Philippa of Hainault, the wife of King Edward III, by Jean Froissart.

RIGHT
Rosemary growing in the kitchen garden at Hampton Court Palace.

36cm
Jenny Malcolm

Strelitzia Reginae

Bird of Paradise

The eye-catching bird of paradise, a flower to turn heads, was actually named in honour of one of our most unshowy consorts, Queen Charlotte.

Charlotte came to Britain from Germany as a teenager in 1761 to wed the young and earnest King George III, with whom she was to have fifteen children over the course of a long and eventful, but for the most part very happy, marriage. The seeds of a passion for botany and collecting rare specimens had been sown early by one of her childhood tutors, but really flourished when it became clear that life as George's Queen, strongly discouraged from any involvement in politics and almost constantly pregnant, offered little outlet for her considerable intelligence.

Royal botanists were far from unprecedented by that time; Charlotte followed in the footsteps of both her husband's mother Augusta, Princess of Wales, and his grandmother Queen Caroline. Both had patronised botanical scholars and between them developed the grounds at Kew Palace – especially Augusta, who had established a dedicated area in the garden for exotic plants, which would eventually evolve into the world-famous Kew Gardens.

By the early 1770s, the royal botanic garden at Kew was under the leadership of its first unofficial director, the naturalist Joseph Banks, and serving as a repository for the variety of new and exotic plant species that were pouring into Britain from the far corners of an expanding empire.

OPPOSITE
The Latin name for the bird of paradise, *Strelitzia reginae*, honours Queen Charlotte of Mecklenburg-Strelitz. By Jenny Malcolm, 2011.

RIGHT
Queen Charlotte, the long-serving consort of King George III, after Thomas Gainsborough, 1781–99.

OPPOSITE
Charlotte had a rustic cottage retreat built in the gardens at Kew in the 1770s. It still stands today.

Banks and Charlotte became friends at around the time that the bird of paradise was 'discovered' by Scottish plant hunter Francis Masson in South Africa and dispatched to Britain, for growing in the hothouses at Kew. But it was not until Banks came to formally classify the flower over ten years later, in 1788, that the plant was given the name of *Strelitzia reginae*, in honour of both the Queen and her birthplace of Mecklenburg Strelitz. (Bird of paradise is the vibrant orange flower's common name, derived from its undeniable resemblance to the head and beak of a tropical bird.)

Naming it for Charlotte was, by then, an obvious choice. In the years that the team had been cultivating the exotic specimen at Kew, she had become an active and influential patron of their work, spending much time there drawing and cataloguing the plants. And her support was undeniably critical to the garden's future success, a fact that cannot have escaped Banks.

The honour came at the very moment where her passion for horticulture began to morph from a mere hobby into her salvation. George III experienced his first episode of so-called 'madness' in 1788, which plunged his wife into a state of distress so acute that it turned the 44-year old Queen's hair completely white. It was to be the first of several times that a sleepless, violent and relentlessly talkative George, agonisingly prone to accusing his wife of adultery and making amorous overtures to her ladies-in-waiting, had to be confined by doctors. And as both his mental state and their marriage crumbled over the following decades, horticulture would provide respite and purpose for his Queen.

At Frogmore House on the Windsor estate, Charlotte made a home for her considerable library and botanical collections. In its sizeable garden, she grew rare and exotic trees and flowers from cuttings sent to her from Kew (possibly including the bird of paradise itself, although there is no evidence to confirm it). Here, too, she sketched, dried and catalogued various new species alongside her daughters, so that as her son took the throne as Regent and her royal duties declined, her reputation for scientific study only increased – and through the Latin name of the bird of paradise, it is preserved for posterity.

ABOVE
Frogmore House, where Charlotte indulged her passion for botany, by William James Bennett after Charles Wild, 1819.

TAGETES

MARIGOLD

Mary, Queen of Scots, as strong willed as her claims to the English throne, chose the cheerful marigold for her personal emblem.

A FLOWER THAT TURNS TO FACE THE SUN, Mary adopted it along with the motto, '*Sa Virtu m'Atire*' ('its virtue draws me'), in her teenage years, and when she married the future King Francis II of France in 1558, at the age of fifteen, the celebratory banners strewn around Paris carried marigolds alongside the French fleurs-de-lys.

After her husband's untimely death just over two years later, Mary returned to Scotland, but, of course, her reign did not last; and when she sought shelter in England in 1568, having been forced to abdicate and flee her kingdom, the marigold remained central to her identity.

Swiftly detained on her arrival by order of her cousin Elizabeth I, who feared Mary's Catholic support and claim to the throne, there were to be many long days of house arrest for the deposed Queen to fill over the coming eighteen-and-a half years, and she turned to needlework. Panels worked on by Mary, now in the collection of the V&A Museum, feature plenty of cheery yellow marigolds. Not just identifiers of the royal creative force behind the panels, they carried a patent message; the sight of the bright little flowers turning their faces towards the sun was generally read as a sign of courage in adversity.

Mary sent her embroidery as gifts to friends and supporters, and placing her particular flower alongside emblems such as the

OPPOSITE
Mary, Queen of Scots, by an unknown artist, c. 1578.

butterfly (a symbol of immortality), and depictions of a hand poised to prune an unfruitful vine (clearly meant to represent the childless Queen Elizabeth), offered her a voice when both her correspondence and movements were being constantly monitored.

And Mary was perhaps not the last monarch to turn to the symbolism of the marigold during a time of captivity. Her grandson Charles I, similarly de-throned, spent just over a year imprisoned at Carisbrooke Castle on the Isle of Wight in the 1640s, and mournful words attributed to him then (with what truth we can't be sure) read:

'The Marigolds observe the Sun
More than my Subjects me have done.'

Perhaps, given its regal history, it was actually rather fitting that in the fashionable 19th-century 'language of flowers' the radiantly colourful and sun-loving marigold was actually considered synonymous with despair.

BELOW AND OPPOSITE
Embroidered panels worked on by Mary, Queen of Scots, which contain identifying symbols and covert statements of resistance. The image below shows marigolds turning towards the sun.

LEFT
The kitchen garden at Hampton Court Palace, where marigold has been used as a companion plant.

ABOVE
King John seals the Magna Carta near the ancient Ankerwycke Yew at Runnymede, by Joseph Martin Kronheim, 1868.

Taxus baccata

Yew

—

Some say the yew is a tree that can live forever, and their resilience against turbulent years is reminiscent of the monarchy's own enduring strength over the centuries.

THOUSANDS OF YEARS OLD, the yew's most ancient specimens pre-date our monarchy, though with their great histories, and amazing ability to renew and revive after periods of apparent decay, they share more than a little similarity with the Crown, whose story has grown alongside theirs.

Over the centuries, yews have imperilled royals: the last Anglo-Saxon King of England, Harold II, is said to have been killed at the Battle of Hastings in 1066 by an arrow fired from a Normon longbow made of yew wood – incredibly strong yet supple, thus ideal for medieval weaponry. And they have protected them: Robert the Bruce, warrior King of the Scots, is believed to have taken shelter, with 200 of his men, under a great yew, already centuries old, on the rocky outcrop of Stuc an t'Iobhairt (the Hill of the Sacrifice), having fled across Loch Lomond after the Battle of Methven in 1306.

Yews have also borne witness to momentous turning points in royal history. Under the branches – or at least in sight of – an enormously stout yew on the bank of the Thames at Runnymede, King John, under pressure from his rebellious barons, set his seal to the Magna Carta in 1215, conceding rights to his people and taking a step towards an established constitution for England. Probably around 1,000 years old already in the 13th century, the Ankerwycke Yew, as it's known, was certainly old enough and big enough to have been a prominent landmark then. The evergreen canopy of the same great tree is said to have shaded Henry VIII as he courted his second wife Anne Boleyn, three centuries later. If that tale is true, it was perhaps not the best omen for their ill-fated union, for thanks to its toxic foliage, the yew has been associated with death as much as immortality. Yews are even known to ooze a deep red, bloodlike sap that would have been all too eerily prescient of the bloody end to Henry and Anne's marriage the following decade. 'O had the Yew its direst venom shed, Upon the cruel Henry's guilty head', the whole story left one 19th-century poet musing.

Yews have also improved the royal view, long being a favourite for topiary, the botanical art form that has its origins in the ancient world and was embraced with enthusiasm in the 16th century. Yews seem to have been among the evergreens trimmed into submission to create the array of ambitious shapes that were admired by a German visitor to Hampton Court Palace in the last years of Elizabeth I's reign: 'men and women, half men and half horse, sirens, serving-maids with baskets, French lilies and delicate crenellations … all true to the life'. And it was Queen Anne who had the palace's famous avenues of yews planted on the East Front in 1707. She intended them to be kept small and carefully clipped, only for them to mushroom into giant beasts under the more relaxed stewardship of Royal Gardener, Lancelot 'Capability' Brown in the late 18th century.

In its decorative form, the yew remains a royal favourite to this day; a pair of imposing topiaries stood at the Great West Door of Westminster Abbey on the day of King Charles' coronation in 2023. They have since been replanted in a new biodiverse topiary garden at Sandringham in Norfolk, home to some 5,000 yews that will be living witnesses to whatever the next few centuries have in store for the royals.

OPPOSITE
The oversized yew trees in Hampton Court Palace's Great Fountain Garden.

Trifolium dubium

Shamrock

Every year on 17th March, St Patrick's Day, a member of the Royal Family greets soldiers of the Irish Guards and presents them with sprigs of shamrock, Ireland's national flower.

THE STORY OF THE SHAMROCK – which takes its name from the Irish *seamair óg*, meaning young shoots of clover – is inextricably entwined with that of St Patrick, the patron saint of the 'Emerald Isle'. Legend has it that when he came to preach the Christian message in the 5th century, he used the three distinct leaves of the little green wildflower, already a symbol of prosperity and good fortune for the Celts, to illustrate the concept of the Holy Trinity, one leaf representing the Father, one the Son, and one the Holy Spirit. Doubts about the veracity of the legend are as abundant as clover is itself in Ireland's green and fertile fields, but the shamrock's fabled link to the revered saint is considered the key to its adoption as the country's national emblem.

The royal tradition of presenting sprigs of shamrock on St Patrick's Day is, however, steeped in no such folklore. It dates back little more than a century to 1901, a year after the Irish Guards were formed by order of Queen Victoria, who wished to honour her Irish soldiers for their bravery in the brutal Boer War, in which their regiments had sustained particularly heavy losses.

OPPOSITE
The late Queen Mother presents shamrocks to the Irish Guards.

Reversing a regulation that had long prohibited either the wearing of 'the green' or its adoption as a regimental emblem

– largely because the shamrock had been a potent symbol of dissent against British rule in Ireland for most of the 19th century – the Queen, in the last year of her reign, permitted all ranks in her Irish regiments and all serving Irish soldiers to wear it every year on St Patrick's Day, to commemorate the gallantry of their countrymen. It is a tradition they keep up to this day, wherever they are in the world.

The first royal presentation of sprigs to the Irish Guards took place after Victoria's death. In 1901 the new Queen Alexandra was the first to send them to soldiers, and within a few years it had become tradition for her to be 'motored to Chelsea Barracks' to make a presentation of sprigs in person. Queen Mary subsequently took up the baton, and the late Queen Mother handed out the shamrock every year between 1966 and her death in 2002. In more recent years the duty has fallen to Catherine, Princess of Wales, who even diligently pins a sprig of shamrock to the collar of the Guards' regimental mascot, a sizeable Irish wolfhound.

As the national emblem of Ireland, the shamrock has, of course, featured in all sorts of other royal ceremonies. Like the rose and thistle, it appears on the Sceptre with Cross presented to the monarch during the coronation ceremony (having been added by George IV in 1820), and it has been woven into the design of the robes and gowns worn by various sovereigns and their consorts on Coronation Day, including the Norman Hartnell-designed dress worn by Elizabeth II in 1953. For good luck, Hartnell is known to have included a four-leaf clover among the clustered shamrocks. The emblem also features alongside the rose and thistle in the Diamond Diadem, the crown created for George IV, which the late Queen wore to every State Opening of Parliament, and in the image that adorned our coins, banknotes and postage stamps during her reign.

OPPOSITE
Catherine, Princess of Wales, now carries out the presentation of shamrocks to the Guards and their mascot, an Irish wolfhound.

OPPOSITE AND ABOVE
Queen Elizabeth II's coronation gown was decorated with the floral emblems of each nation of Great Britain.

RIGHT
A mass of tulips on the East Front of Hampton Court Palace, which was added for William and Mary.

TULIPA

TULIP

After the 'Glorious Revolution' of 1688, the royal garden at Hampton Court Palace was flush with tulips, satisfying flower-loving Queen Mary II's desire for fresh, cut blooms.

THE SPRING TULIP WAS STILL SOMETHING OF A STATUS SYMBOL by the time she and her husband, the Dutch ruler, William of Orange, ascended to the throne as joint sovereigns. The so-called 'tulip mania' of the 1630s – when in Holland single bulbs of the choicest varieties had changed hands for the price of a comfortable house, before the market spectacularly crashed – had long since subsided. However, tulips – which were only introduced to England from the Middle East, via Vienna, in the 1570s – remained a fashionable flower, and their bulbs were still expensive to procure.

With the Dutch so besotted by the tulip, and their growers fast cornering the market for bulbs, having a passion for the elegant blooms was more or less a patriotic duty for William and Mary. Like many of their more exotic plants, they brought tulips to England with them, where they were planted at Hampton Court Palace – though not as we are used to seeing them. Today, tulips are considered at their most beautiful when they carpet the ground in an explosion of colour, but 17th-century taste said individual tulips were made to be seen and admired from all sides. Gardeners marvelling at their distinctive form thus preferred to plant just handfuls of bulbs together, placing each group around 18–24in apart, a sizeable planting distance by modern standards.

The tulips that filled the gardens at Hampton Court in spring probably included the finely striped varieties that were the most desirable (gardeners would not fully identify until the 1930s that the 'flamed' appearance so admired was actually caused by a virus, spread by aphids). They were largely grown to satisfy the Queen's demand for cut flowers wherever she was in residence. Seemingly evangelical about fresh blooms, knowledgeable botanist Mary adorned her garden rooms with them, possibly displaying them in blue-and-white pyramid vases.

These tall ceramic vessels had a series of spouts, which could be filled with damp moss to showcase cut stems indoors. Her own innovation, and a collision of her two great passions in life, horticulture and ceramics, most of these glazed vases were made for the Queen in Delft in the Netherlands.

Tulips remained a staple of the Hampton Court gardens even after Mary died from smallpox in 1694, at the age of just thirty-two, particularly in the Privy Garden. And today, of course, the palace celebrates the centuries of cultivation with an annual Tulip Festival in April, when thousands of the former Queen's favoured flowers burst into bloom, and gardeners are on-hand to provide growing tips to those who fancy adorning their own house and gardens as she did.

OPPOSITE
Tulips still provide a splash of spring colour in the gardens at Hampton Court today.

ABOVE AND OPPOSITE
Tulips feature in the decorative schemes inside William and Mary's baroque apartments at Hampton Court Palace.

VIOLA

VIOLET

Its sweet scent has made the violet enduringly popular, but it has also featured prominently in the lives of the royals, from funeral processions to medicinal treatments.

THE DAY OF PRINCE ALBERT'S FUNERAL in December 1861 was cold and wintry, the sky a leaden grey. As a mournful procession of carriages made their way from Windsor Castle's Upper Ward for the 'last sad ceremony' in St George's Chapel, the scene was shrouded in black. A splash of colour came courtesy of the violets resting on top of his coffin; a bouquet of them, with a single white camellia in the centre, from his bereft wife Queen Victoria, and three moss and violet wreaths, sent by three of their daughters, Alice, Helena and Louise.

Albert's death at the age of just forty-two had been sudden and unexpected, and the arrangements for the ceremony at Windsor were made quickly. But though flowers were not yet an established part of funeral custom, it's likely that the choice of violets to adorn his coffin was a significant one. The delicate purple blooms have a long association with death and mourning; both the Greeks and the Romans are said to have placed violets about the graves and tombs of their dead. Violets had been symbolic of constancy and faithfulness for centuries, too, making them a poignant offering from a devoted widow.

Albert's violets were brought by train from Osborne House in the company of the chief royal mourners, and were sent to the funeral with the blessing of Victoria, who did not attend

OPPOSITE
Violets have long been symbolic of constancy and faithfulness. By Margaret Hatherley Champ, 2010.

herself – not because she was prostrate with grief (though she was), but because funerals were considered no place for ladies of genteel birth, who were not trusted to be able to control their emotions in public. The violets were thus her envoy.

Yet though her consort's death sunk the Queen into a deep depression from which she took decades to recover, violets clearly retained no sorrowful associations for her. Far from it, in fact. She continued to delight in the spring showing of them at Windsor and Osborne, recording in her diary when they were 'smelling so sweet', or when she had given or received nosegays of violets.

They were not a universal royal favourite, however. On his restoration to the throne after the defeat of Napoleon Bonaparte in 1815, King Louis XVIII of France attempted to supress the wearing of violets and the creation of any images of them, as the humble flower, a favourite of Bonaparte's first wife Joséphine, had become an emblem of fidelity to the former emperor. But Britain's Tudor monarchs had uses for both violets and their heart-shaped leaves; a recipe for a topical compound devised by Henry VIII, probably for the leg ulcers that followed a severe jousting accident, called for the latter.

The sweet – if fleeting – scent of the violet was partly responsible for their surge in popularity during Victoria's reign; small posies were sold cheaply on street corners as an antidote to the unpleasant smells that swirled around 19th-century cities. Violets were a favourite for buttonholes, and adorned ladies' hats, the fashion fuelled by the known partiality of both the Queen and her daughter-in-law Princess Alexandra. The Princess was often seen with a cluster pinned to her clothing, and during the reign of her husband Edward VII, thousands of them were cultivated under forcing frames in the gardens at Windsor and Sandringham. And, if some of the newspapers are to be believed, when Edward died in 1910, Alexandra, like Victoria before her, turned to violets, picking the flower for her funeral cross.

OPPOSITE
The walled garden of Osborne House, with violets featuring prominently in the foreground.

ABOVE
Violets grown at Osborne House were taken to Windsor for Prince Albert's funeral on 23 December 1861.

OPPOSITE
Albert's funeral procession heads to St George's Chapel in Windsor Castle. Illustration from *The Life and Times of Queen Victoria*, c. 1901.

FUNERAL OF THE PRINCE CONSORT: ARRIVAL AT ST. GEORGE'S CHAPEL.

ABOVE
Illustration of a pansy from Basilius Besler's *Hortus Eystettensis*, 1613.

Viola Tricolor

Pansy

The modest pansy, a welcome burst of colour in the winter months, was the flower Queen Elizabeth I loved best.

With a name that punned with the French word *pensée,* meaning 'thought', in 16th-century England the pretty yellow and purple pansy said 'think of me' – especially in a romantic sense, as reflected in the other names it commonly went by, 'heartsease' and 'love-in-idleness'.

As an eleven-year-old princess, Elizabeth certainly appears to have intended her father Henry VIII, and his sixth wife Katherine Parr, to think of her, and more specifically perhaps to think about bringing her to court more permanently, when they received the handwritten volumes of translation she bound and dotted with delicately embroidered pansies as gifts for them on New Year's Eve, 1544.

Once she became Queen, fourteen years later, her favourite flowers featured frequently in her wardrobe, and consequently in her portraiture; pansies pepper her bodice in the famous 'Rainbow' portrait, and are among the symbols scattered across her dress in the 'Hardwick' portrait. The pansy naturally also featured on the sumptuous gifts which courtiers were expected to present to their sovereign at New Year; 'Bess' of Hardwick – who probably commissioned the portrait – chose for her Queen a blue satin cloak embroidered with pansies in 1576, which was said to have gone down particularly well.

No doubt the romantic symbolism of the pansy – the wild, native variety, without the trademark blotches which came only as a result of 19th-century cross-breeding – appealed to the older and more assured Elizabeth. Its three petals were popularly read during her reign as a lady flanked by two aspiring lovers, and the 'Virgin Queen' was nothing if not hugely successful at encouraging suitors, royal and otherwise, while always eluding them.

ABOVE AND OPPOSITE
The 'Rainbow Portrait' of Queen Elizabeth I, and detail of the bodice, embroidered with pansies, gillyflowers and sprigs of honeysuckle. Unknown artist, c. 1600–3.

ABOVE
King George III in 1785,
by Thomas Gainsborough.

Vitis

Grape Vine

The world's biggest grape vine was planted for King George III to provide fruit for the royal table, and more than 250 years on, it is still growing strong in the gardens at Hampton Court Palace.

Although vines had formed part of the palace's grounds in the 17th century, the 'Great Vine' (as it became known) was planted from a small cutting in 1768 by Lancelot 'Capability' Brown, then a royal gardener to George III. It is one of few identifiable changes that the celebrated Brown made to the gardens at Hampton Court. He may have been acting on his own initiative, or perhaps on the wishes of George and his wife Charlotte – grapes were a popular choice for the Georgian dessert course, though only for the upper classes, because they were labour-intensive to cultivate and thus expensive. When the *Gentleman's Magazine* ran a short item on the King's vine in 1798, one of the key facts it imparted to its readers was that its abundant bunches of grapes were estimated to be 'worth altogether at least £400' – about four times what a reasonably affluent tradesman of the period earned in an entire year.

It was thriving, and already a curiosity, when the 18th century drew to a close, despite the fact that the wider gardens at Hampton Court were looking outmoded, with Brown having been accused of neglecting his royal patch. The vine, which grows from just a single plant and produces dessert grapes of the sweet Black Hamburg variety, had, in fact, flourished from its first introduction – it had benefitted from the fertile ground in which it was planted, near the site of the palace's old Tudor latrines!

Over the centuries the Great Vine has had extraordinary care. The first of many designated Vine Keepers was appointed more than 150 years ago, and given a cottage right next door, so that they would be on hand to water it, monitor the temperature, and increase or decrease the ventilation in the vine house. They guarded the fruits of their labour closely; each bunch of grapes was numbered, and sampling strictly forbidden.

For the greater part of its life, grapes from the vine have been reserved exclusively for the royal table. According to an early 19th-century chronicler, George III enjoyed the fruits of the Hampton Court vine for half a century, though his son George IV, the writer added sardonically, 'preferred the manufactured juice of the grape, to that which was matured and evolved by nature'. Although Queen Victoria had no use for Hampton Court Palace and is credited with opening up the gardens to the public in 1838, she continued to have the vine's juicy crop sent to her at Windsor or Osborne House. At this time, it was reportedly anywhere between 1,200 and 2,500 bunches. Only in the early years of the 20th century did her son Edward VII decide that the vine's produce was surplus to royal requirements and give permission for its grapes to be sold.

By that time, on account of its age and ever-increasing size, the vine was just as much of a tourist attraction as the palace's hedge maze or Old Master paintings, if not more. A purpose-built viewing cabin was opened in 1906 to ease the queues of hundreds of thousands of visitors who came to take a look every year.

Today, two and half centuries since it was planted, the size of the Great Vine – which has branches stretching 130ft – makes it a world record holder. And its fruit, once forbidden to all but royal plates, is now usually available for the public to carry home from the palace gift shop.

ABOVE
The Great Vine as it looked in 1840, shortly after Hampton Court Palace was first opened to the public.

OVERLEAF LEFT
Members of the public watch from the viewing cabin as grapes from the vine are harvested.

OVERLEAF RIGHT
The grapes of the Black Hamburg variety, as grown on the Great Vine, by E. D. Smith.

Black Hamburg Grape. IX

S. Watts sculp[t]

INDEX

AUTHOR ACKNOWLEDGEMENTS

Thanks are due to a number of people who have worked hard to bring this book to life: to Clare Murphy, Sebastian Edwards and the gardeners at Historic Royal Palaces who generously shared their time and knowledge, to their counterparts at English Heritage and the Royal Collection Trust who helped with additional information, and to Heather Boisseau and Matt Tomlinson at Headline, who ably steered it through the editorial and production process.

PICTURE CREDITS

The publishers would like to thank the following sources for their kind permission to reproduce the pictures in this book.

ALAMY STOCK PHOTO: Album 18, 106, 203; A. Amsel 152; Ann Ronan Picture Library/Photo 12 30-31; Antiqua Print Gallery 172; Art Collection 3 109; Chris Aubrey 179 top; Chronicle 139; eye35.pix 88, 120-121; Florilegius 84, 134; Fiona Hanson/PA Images 59 top; GL Archive 144; Gallery Of Art 122; gillsbowen/Stockimo 111; Günter Gräfenhain/mauritius images GmbH 192; John Hammond/The National Trust Photolibrary 168, 169; IanDagnall Computing 115, 138, 151, 166, 198; Iconographic Archive 148; incamerastock 42, 112, 157; Christopher Ison 179 bottom; JJs 194; Justin Kase ztwoz 191; Keystone Press 176; Le Pictorium/Active Museum/Active Art 110; Yui Mok/PA Images 133; OBNW 59 bottom; PA Images 53, 55; Peakscape 123 right; The Picture Art Collection 70, 100; Pictures Now 196; Science History Images 12; Mick Sharp 21; Signal Photos 197; Trinity Mirror/Mirrorpix 140; WENN Rights Ltd 124; World History Archive 89. **BRIDGEMAN IMAGES:** Agnew's, London 20; British Library archive 75, 105 bottom; Natural History Museum, London 36; Private Collection 87; Royal Collection Trust/© His Majesty King Charles III, 2024 28, 48. **GETTY IMAGES:** De Agostini Picture Library 24, 102; Fine Art Images/Heritage Images 101; Florilegius/Universal Images Group 23, 56, 66, 69, 72, 78, 116, 154; Highgrove Enterprises 63; Historica Graphica Collection/Heritage Images 22; Historical Picture Archive/Corbis 39, 147; Hulton Archive 137; Keystone/Hulton Archive 81; Keystone-France/Gamma-Keystone 15; Danny Lawson/AFP 10; mikroman6 4, 123 left; Museum of London/Heritage Images 29; Tim Graham Picture Library 60, 130; Ian West/AFP 50. **HISTORIC ROYAL PALACES:** 9, 32, 35, 40, 41, 45, 49, 64, 76–7, 82, 88, 90, 93, 94–5, 96, 114–5, 119, 127, 128–9, 143, 158–9, 160, 162, 163, 165, 170–1 (Photo by Aerial Vue), 175, 182, 185, 186, 187, 188, 193, 201, 202. **ROYAL COLLECTION TRUST:** 27, 46, 54, 83, 104–5, 180–1. **SHUTTERSTOCK:** Jonathan Brady/WPA Pool 16; James Gray/Daily Mail 71; PJ photography 17. **WIKIMEDIA COMMONS:** Private Collection 67, 99.